A Kodiak Bear Mauling

Living and Dying
with Alaska's Bears

D1562456

Terror Bay

By R. Keith Rogan

With Gratitude to Chuck, Brian and Ira.
Without their courage, skills and ingenuity I
would not be alive to write this book.

Copyright 2013 R. Keith Rogan
All rights reserved to the author.
ISBN: 1470082896
ISBN 13: 9781470082895

Paperback edition published 2013 by Terror
Bay Publishing

All images copyright Adina Preston
Photography or Terror Bay Publishing,
respectively

Cover Design By
Adina Preston Photography & Graphic Design
www.adinaprestondesign.com

Contents

Chapter 1

The Eyes of a Grizzly

I was moving very slowly and quietly with the wind in my face and as I rounded a clump of brush, I looked to my left and saw a bear lying there. She was perhaps ten yards away and looking me right in the eye, crouched low to the ground with her paws in front ready to pounce. I have often wondered what would have happened if our eyes had not met. Would the animal have allowed me to go in peace, or just taken me down from behind after I passed? As it was, the bear just leaped upon eye contact and was inside the swing of my rifle before I could get it up to my shoulder. The next few minutes would change my life forever, leaving physical and mental scars that still plague me to this day.

Meeting the eyes of a grizzly is an interesting experience because those eyes hold real intelligence and power. The eyes of other common Alaskan animals such as moose or caribou reveal little beyond fear or vague curiosity. A ruminant's brain has very little room for much beyond eating, fleeing and mating. Your attention is drawn to other things on such an animal, the antlers perhaps...

A bear is a different proposition altogether. The wide brown eyes of this predator are expressive and calculating and meeting them is to know that you are looking into the mind of a thinking animal. I cannot stress that difference enough, though it is difficult to articulate this to people who have not had the experience. When meeting a grizzly at close range you generally find yourself waiting for the animal to make a decision - to leave, hopefully. Your eyes will lock with those of the bear and there will be some sort of visceral communication taking place. You can watch the play of emotion and calculation cross the animals face while he evaluates you and tries to decide what your presence means and what he should do about it.

Are you a threat? Are you food? Can he take those succulent salmon or berries you are holding?

Those eyes may show surprise at first, followed by curiosity (examining you or the fish or berries you carry), to anger, bluster, intimidation, indecision... What you do to influence that animal's next move may hold the key to how this little drama plays out; whether you go home with a great bear tale or become organic matter feeding the salmonberries and wild roses.

Reading the animals intent takes no particular skill or insight; indeed, the animal's entire face and upper body has evolved into a useful communication tool capable of broadcasting some fairly complex (and quite unmistakable) messages. The facial anatomy of a bear mirrors many of the same expressive features as that of a man, and those expressions can be understood in the same way. At its most basic level, the face can meet yours in challenge, or look down or away to show submission or non-threatening intent. To express more complex emotions; the brows can raise, wrinkle or narrow to denote surprise, curiosity or anger. The mouth and lips can open to form an "O" of contentment, or curl back to bare teeth in anger or threat. The muscles of the upper body and neck can be instantly "pumped up" to form a threat display that any body-builder would understand and envy; the fur over that massive frame rising like that of a cat to enhance the menacing posture.

The animal will accentuate those visual cues with a wide range of vocalizations. It can use everything from a questioning or neutral "chuffing" to ever louder (and more threatening) snarls and roars, leading up to a very fearful "clicking" or "clacking" noise made by snapping its teeth together; a clear demonstration of the power of its massive jaws, and of its willingness to use them if necessary.

The face changes when the animal reaches a decision. Most often, the bear will simply exhibit a dismissive expression and posture, relaxing its features and upper body muscula-ture before turning its gaze away and leaving in peace.

On very rare occasions, they will decide on another course of action. Not many people have seen the eyes of an attacking grizzly, and many who have are no longer able to tell anyone what they looked like. I can tell you that those eyes show nothing but cold anger and grim determi-nation. The face of an attacking bear is all busi-ness - a cold expressionless mask. Adrenaline enlarges the bear's pupils until they cover the lighter iris, turning the eye into a lifeless black orb shining brightly from between narrowed lids. The ears fall flat against the head and the skin of the entire face draws back tightly against the skull. The animal simply begins running at 35 miles per hour straight at the object of its anger. Still, there is a message to be read here; a short ursine memo under the subject header; "I Am Going to Kill You Now" followed by the brief reminder that it is nothing personal...

The Kodiak archipelago is tucked within the long reach of the Alaskan coast like a group of badly behaved children in the arms of a somewhat aloof mother. Thumbing its nose at the latitude of its arctic parent, cheeky Kodiak bathes in the waters of warm southern currents that give the island a temperate maritime climate seemingly more appropriate to locales far to the south.

In the same way that the Gulf Stream warms the British Isles, the Kuroshio Current begins in warmer latitudes far to the south to move northward along the rim of the Pacific and then east to the Gulf of Alaska to surround Kodiak with a warm wet noose. Above this warm river in the cold northern sea is another warm river of moist low-pressure air. These warm sea currents and air masses move north to collide with much colder waters and arctic high-pressure air along the Aleutian Islands. This remote island chain marks the boundary between the genteel Pacific and its rowdy and temperamental arctic neighbor, the Bering Sea. The enormous temperature and pressure extremes in this "Birthplace of the Winds" spawn a seemingly endless series of cyclonic low-pressure storms that spin to the northeast to lash Kodiak with the rain and fog which envelope it for much of the year.

That wet marine climate ends abruptly when it meets the high coastal mountains ringing the Alaska mainland. Beyond that point is the true arctic – the land of Iditarod and Jack London, of clear skies and the Aurora Borealis.

In winter, while mainland Alaska is covered in deep snow, Kodiak is glistening in the fog and seemingly endless winter rains: mildewed perhaps, but generally ice free at sea level for much of the winter. This winter moisture is what makes the island group the rich land that it is, drenching the lower elevations with misty rains and piling up as deep snow in the mountains to replenish the myriad rivers and streams through the dryer summer months. In turn, those clear mountain streams rush down to provide spawning grounds for the hundreds of millions of salmon that annually return to the islands in the age-old cycle.

Kodiak is not only biologically rich, but also beautiful almost beyond description. On a sunny summer day one can be struck by the almost tropical aspect of the islands. Wildflowers grow in profusion here which have to be seen to be believed - damp bogs explode with purple iris and exotic chocolate lilies and even its own variety of orchid, while above, the higher slopes host a profusion of fireweed or lupines that can turn whole hillsides pink or purple overnight. On warm July days, mountain meadows perfume the air for a mile around when the wild roses open their short-lived and pungent blossoms. Belts of salmonberries, huckleberries and high bush cranberries are always in sight, offering delicious fruit that can be gathered almost effortlessly. From a distance, the grasses appear to clothe the mountainsides like vertical golf courses, a green that hurts the eye, a green so intense that photographers are sometimes accused of tinting pictures taken in early summer.

Chunky bodied blacktail deer forage through the richness on their delicate legs, building up layers of fat to get them through the leaner days of winter. Massive Roosevelt elk bugle from the forested regions of Afognak and Raspberry islands. Mountain goats dance improbably along high precipices, seemingly in defiance of gravity. Whales of many different varieties can be observed from any headland by a patient watcher, their white plumes standing out against the dark blue summer sea. Soaring eagles drift lazily on the warm air currents. Thousands of songbirds fill the air with sound. Fat bees hum drowsily among the flowers. Rivers and streams are choked with millions of spawning salmon.

It's difficult to describe to a stranger what Kodiak actually looks like since traveling only a few miles in any direction will generally reveal an entirely different topography. The northeastern section of the island group is heavily forested with stands of massive Sitka Spruce that shut out all sunlight, creating a twilight world of green moss and eerie silence; a temperate rainforest. Snow capped peaks dominate much of the center of the island group, standing guard over steep grassy slopes. Other areas (particularly in the south) are made up of low hills covered with scrubby brush, country resembling eastern Wyoming in a damp spring. Moving to the coast, you find miles of volcanic black sand beaches interspersed with high cliffs against which the North Pacific crashes, slowly eating away the defiant land; an epic battle that will someday be lost to the eternal sea. Deep fiords are carved into the interior so that no place on the island is far from salt water.

Perhaps the most typical Kodiak vista would be a scene of grassy mountainsides cut with thick stands of the ubiquitous red alder, a low shrubby tree that forms dense impenetrable tangles that are best avoided by bipeds. One quickly learns that in Kodiak a straight line is not necessarily the shortest distance between two points, if that line intersects an alder belt!

Those same alders are the first harbingers of spring. As the days begin to lengthen, you might notice the green growth of the hardy wild parsnip or "pushky" dotting the brown hillsides as early as late March, and you might think the endless rains of winter are over, the endless summer days right around the corner... a forlorn hope. It will not be until sometime in May or even early June, when the alders announce that summer has come. The buds of the red alder will not be tempted to open until the first warm days, no matter how late in the season that is. When they do open it will happen literally overnight; one day you are looking at bare brown winter hills and on the next, they are shot with the vibrant green of young alder leaves tracing their way up the mountainsides like arteries carrying life to a living body. Within a few days of that first alder greenery, the grasses will shoot up to cover the last dead growth of the previous year; filling in the remaining slopes to create a lush green world. That first burst of greenery is an almost embarrassing and improbable lime-green; a fruity, tropical and effeminate color which will only gradually darken to a green suitable to the staid northern world - Ireland in the North Pacific.

Summer is here and the pace of life will become frenetic for all living things.

In these latitudes, the summer sun does not simply cross the sky from east to west, but rather describes a parabola, rising in the north to go *around* the sky until eventually it sinks below the northern horizon again, a few degrees west of where it rose that morning. It stays there just below the horizon, lighting the sky and leaving the earth in twilight for a few hours, until rising again to turn the morning dew into ground-clinging mist that can pour down the valleys like ethereal rivers. The near endless daylight is often disorienting to the newcomer, interfering with sleep patterns and leading to increased energy and activity, and often mental confusion when exhaustion steps in like a loan shark come to collect payment. Much of this is a physiological response to the increased output of endorphins (and a host of other chemicals) produced by the endocrine system. It is rather like Seasonal Affective Disorder (the "Christmas Blues") in reverse; an elevation of mood caused by an excess of chemical soup dumped into the bloodstream in response to the increased sunlight, rather than the shortage of those same chemicals created by the lack of sunlight in winter. You really do have more energy and require less sleep in the northern summer and that same furious burst of activity can be seen in the other living things around you.

It is a mistake to allow yourself to be lulled into carelessness by the heady beauty of this verdant landscape, or by the apparently tame and tranquil nature of the wildlife busily storing up calories for the winter, almost heedless of the presence of man. One must always keep in mind that just around the next bend in the stream or lying amid that patch of wild roses may lurk the largest land-predator on earth. It is a heart-stopping moment when a formless mass in the brush alongside the trail materializes into the shape of a giant bear. Invariably, it is already watching you well before your weaker senses become aware of him.

The islands are home to about three thousand brown (Kodiak) bears, or about one bear per square mile. Think about that.

In strictly mathematical terms, the odds are that wherever you stand on these islands, a circle drawn around your figure reaching out one half mile in every direction will likely hold a grizzly. Of course, all of this depends on where you are standing and at what time of year. A circle drawn within a bend of the Karluk River in July (when the salmon are running in force) might include fifty bears. A much larger circle drawn there in December when the bears have retreated to the hills to prepare for the long sleep might include none.

The "Kodiak" brown bear is not a species unto itself, but a mammoth version of the grizzly; the same bear once common to most of the North American continent. Male grizzlies in the interior of Alaska or the Canadian Yukon (where protein is relatively scarce), average a mere three hundred pounds in weight (figures verified by official sampling of hunter trophies). Grizzlies in Wyoming and Montana are somewhat larger, averaging closer to five hundred pounds. Contrast those sizes with coastal Alaskan grizzlies (to include those on Kodiak) that can reach fifteen hundred pounds or perhaps even larger if field reports are to be believed. The problem with weighing such critters is they simply will not cooperate unless you shoot them first, and then they are too large to drag to a scale. Since there are very few roads on Kodiak or the adjacent coastal regions, trophies are not loaded onto a convenient pickup truck and taken into town to be weighed, but must be skinned and butchered in the field. With no scales out in the wilderness (where the largest bears are taken), the size becomes subjective and sometimes inflated.

A friend of mine shot a good sized fall bear on a ranch near town and that bear was hauled onto a cattle scale and found to weigh just over eleven hundred pounds. Many years ago, the crew of a salmon tender in a remote Kodiak bay shot a large bear. That bear was pulled onto the fish scales and (according to numerous witnesses) weighed over eighteen hundred pounds! These are exceptional animals. Biologists tell us that good sized male "Kodiak" bears generally weigh somewhere just shy of a thousand pounds while larger trophy class specimens might go over twelve hundred. Females (of all species of bear) weigh about two thirds that of the males.

It is a little more complicated than an excess of food in the lush coastal regions creating larger bears. Rather, it is a survival adaptation resulting from thousands of generations of natural selection. For example, in this nutrient-rich environment the largest bear can muscle its way to the best fishing spot or bully a smaller adversary away from a sow in heat to pass along its genes. Natural selection simply favors the larger animal.

In the bleak mountains of interior Alaska, a bear that size would be hard put to find enough fuel to feed such a body. Indeed, depending on the habitat, interior grizzlies may require from ten to one hundred square miles (per bear) to find enough forage to survive. Moreover, with such a low population density, merely *finding* a mate is a great challenge and added size bestows no advantage. Natural selection favors the smaller animal and those genes are the ones passed along. Same bear, different adaptations.

So, we find ourselves on this lush island, densely populated with enormous grizzly bears and we have to ask ourselves a question; how dangerous is that? The answer is, not as dangerous as you would think. The very richness that makes such a profuse number of enormous critters possible also keeps them fat, happy and relatively even-tempered. Ask any biologist or guide familiar with both mountain and coastal grizzlies to opine about the relative dangers of these ursine cousins and they will uniformly tell you that the smaller mountain animal is much more unpredictable and dangerous. Much like dogs, the hungry and stressed animal is much more likely to bite you than the sleek and well-fed family pet.

For the most part, we weak and puny humans can wander these wild islands in relative safety. The bears generally behave themselves and react by avoiding us, while the wise human gives the bear the same courtesy. Bears just become part of the landscape to the local, after-dinner talk rather than a life or death experience. Complacency rules the day.

Humans and bears have a long history of co-existence on Kodiak. Archeological digs reveal that humans have lived here continuously for 10,000 years and possibly much longer. Indeed, some places show a record of continuous habitation rivaling sites anywhere in the world. The village of Karluk (for example), dates back 7000 years – older than any city in Europe and all but a few in the Middle East. The Koniag/ Alutiiq people have always lived comfortably with the bears. While the bears hold a prominent place in the mythology, their skins were also prized as blankets and carpets, their meat as valuable nutrition. The animal was respected for its power and intelligence, but also valued as a simple resource. The old tales often revolve around the similarities between bears and humans, or their ability to adopt human form or vice versa. Largely though, the Koniag were people who looked to the sea for all things - perhaps a man unafraid to challenge a whale from a tiny kayak is less awestruck by a giant bear than you or I? The bear policy was largely live and let live, and remains so today.

When the Russians came, they too seemed largely uninterested in the bears. Like the Koniag, they looked to the sea (in particular to the ubiquitous and valuable sea otter), for a living. The bears were occasionally hunted and surely, no visiting dignitary could go home without his prized bear rug, but beyond that, little attention was given to them. A bears hide was worth only $1/10^{th}$ that of a sea otter, and was much more difficult and dangerous to procure with the primitive firearms of the day.

It was not until the early part of the twentieth century (when under American control) and salmon canneries began to dot the remote bays of Kodiak that people began to take notice. By that time, the bears had been catalogued and described by biologists as the "largest land predator on earth" (or similar superlatives), which led sportsmen around the world to add the creature to their list of desired trophies. Meanwhile, Alaskan fishermen merely considered them competitors for the salmon and often shot them on sight. Some hunted them for the valuable hides in their off time or chartered as guides to take teams of sport hunters out after the salmon season wound down. Protective regulations were issued in 1901 and again in 1925 when all commercial hide hunting was banned. Still, this was (and is) a remote place and there was no real enforcement of such laws. It was not until 1941 with the creation of the Kodiak National Wildlife Refuge (encompassing most of the island group), that the bears were given real protection. Bear hunting is still allowed on the refuge, but it is tightly controlled and bear populations have never been larger or healthier. Hunters and tourists pour millions of dollars into the Alaskan economy and we have come full circle to again reach a place where bears are both respected for their beauty and power yet regarded as a valuable resource, and protected as such.

Kodiak today is not greatly different than it was a hundred years ago. A small area on the northeast end of the main island holds the city of Kodiak, and a very limited road system. The rest of the island group remains roadless and wild, accessible only by floatplane or boat. A few tiny native villages can be found here and there, still holding on to many of the time-honored traditions of an older world.

The remoteness and lack of road access makes Kodiak an expensive proposition for tourists and sportsmen. To get out into the refuge requires an expensive commuter flight from Anchorage followed by an even more expensive charter flight via floatplane from the city of Kodiak out into the refuge. Not many are willing to make the financial sacrifice or put up with the many inconveniences of such a trip, and that fact keeps the refuge from turning into the "Disneyland" destination that has befallen the Kenai and other easily accessible destinations around the state.

Those that do make the trip are in for a real treat. The refuge is a wonderful place. Two large rivers at the south end offer some of the best

King salmon fishing in the world. All the rivers and streams of the island offer great fishing for at least one of the five varieties of pacific salmon, as well as trout, char (Dolly Varden), steelhead, etc. Giant Pacific halibut can be fished offshore. The Sitka Blacktail deer, mountain goats and Roosevelt elk draw a growing number of hunters. In addition, of course, an ever-increasing number of eco-tourists come to simply view and photograph the wildlife and otherwise enjoy the wilderness experience. None of these people need be crowded by the presence of others; the refuge is large enough for all of them to find complete solitude if they so desire.

Recreating in such remote and dangerous country is a gratifying experience though it must be recognized that some types of recreation (almost inevitably) may lead you into conflict with our ursine neighbors. Campers frequently draw bears, sometimes intentionally leaving food out for photo opportunities and actually train bears to approach campsites. The same salmon runs that draw anglers also draw bears, and while a wise man simply moves to another spot when a bear shows up, you will often see photos of anglers standing a few yards from bears without apparent conflict. I would argue that such practices (if nothing else) inure the bears to our presence and open the door to future problems for the animal (and the people it may approach) having once lost its wariness of humans.

There is no central repository for data on bear attacks. Since my own mauling several years ago, I have followed the subject with some interest. In Alaska alone there are anywhere from five to ten attacks per year reported in local newspapers. No one can know how many unexplained disappearances of hikers and hunters (and there are many) might also be due to bears. Moreover, nobody knows how many bears might be shot in legitimate self-defense and left unreported due to fear of legal entanglements. Perhaps just as importantly, nobody really knows how many bears are shot and killed (or merely injured), for such illegitimate reasons as "it was too close." Many (if not most), bears killed and recovered after attacking a human are found to have previous injuries which contributed to its subsequent behavior. An injured bear is a dangerous bear and so oddly enough, the unreasoning fear of bears can create a real reason to fear bears when as so often happens, they are wounded by frightened people.

ADINA PRESTON
Photography
Graphic Design

As far back as she can remember, Adina has been motivated to capture a sense of beauty and art from her surroundings and to translate that into her design and photography work. In the thriving arts scene of her native Bucharest, she was intrigued by the play of light and shadow across the eclectic mix of neoclassical, Bauhaus and Art Deco in her beautiful old city. She honed her skills capturing the various moods of Bucharest; the somber grays of winter, the bright summer markets and interesting faces, and life going on around her.

Later, in Miami, she found herself captivated by the bright tropical light and colors of south Florida and had to discover an entirely new palette to document this scene. Now living in Kodiak, Adina has found a new and mysterious northern light to capture. The strange light, shadows and mists of this ruggedly beautiful island are often best captured in classic black and white photography. Adina has been kind enough to contribute this section to illustrate the beauty of Kodiak in ways that my mere words cannot convey.

Please enjoy Kodiak as viewed through the lens of Adina Preston!

R. Keith Rogan

Adina received her Bachelor of Arts in Marketing and Management in Bucharest, and has worked as a freelance designer and photographer since 2008. Her portfolio can be viewed at adinaprestondesign.com. Her prints can be purchased at adinaprestonphotography.smugmug.com.

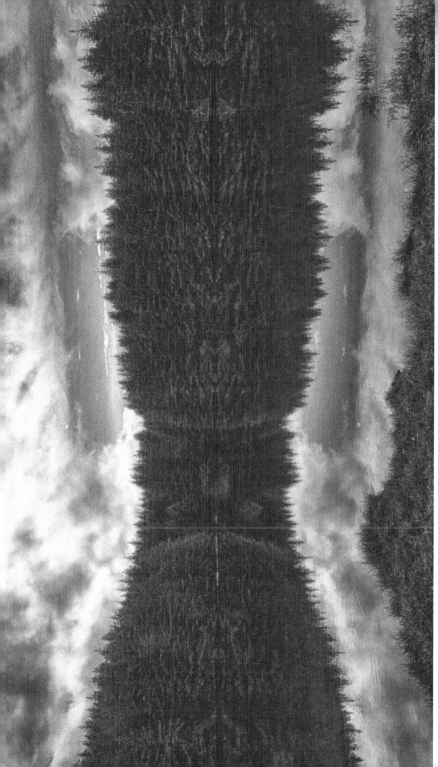

Chapter 2
About Bears

To understand these animals better, it will be necessary to draw a general outline of the species. It is not my intention to present a biology thesis here, the information presented is intended only to give the reader a very general knowledge of the animal and its habits. I am not a biologist, but have drawn much of the following from the best information available. All of the following is colored by my own experiences and observations, such as they are. The following information is applicable to coastal brown/grizzly bears. Most of the information will also apply to inland grizzlies and to a much lesser extent, black bears, which are quite a different animal altogether.

The brown bear (ursus arctos) has the widest distribution of any species of bear. It was once found across most of the northern hemisphere, from Western Europe through Asia and thence into North America down to central Mexico. Within that wide range, various sub-species have adapted to habitats as diverse as the arctic plain, sub-tropical forests, coastal rain forests, alpine tundra and even the deserts of northern Mexico. The largest sub-species are the coastal brown bears found along the Pacific coast of Alaska and in the very similar habitat of the neighboring Kamchatka peninsula in the Russian Far East.

The Kodiak sub-species is Ursus Arctos Middendorfi. These coastal brown bears rival the polar bear as the largest land predators on the planet, though which one is worthy of the title is somewhat subjective. In terms of weight, the brown bear is probably the larger, but by body measurement, the lankier polar bear takes the prize. Take your pick.

I have to take a moment here to put the size of a coastal brown bear into a perspective that the average person can grasp. When speaking of mature brown bears you will often see them described in general terms as a "ten foot bear," or that such an animal stands "ten feet tall." As large as that sounds, this actually sells the animal short because most people misunderstand the term and use it incorrectly. The term "ten foot bear" comes from sporting organizations that use the square foot of the hide as general guideline to separate a trophy class bear from smaller animals. A hide is "squared" by measuring from front claw tip to front claw tip and then from snout to tail, adding the two figures together and then dividing by two. In very rough terms, you can think of a ten-foot bear as one that measures ten feet from nose to tail. Therefore, when that ten foot bear stands on his hind legs he is closer to thirteen feet in height! Look around you and find a standard door seven feet in height, now if you mentally double that and realize that a brown bear standing on his hind legs approaches that size, you'll begin to understand how very large these animals are. Imagine such an animal rising from the brush alongside the trail to glare at you with an angry expression... imagine what your shorts might look like after such an event.

Of course, brown bears are quadrupeds and are generally viewed standing on all four feet (rather than towering on two legs to foul the underpants of surprised anglers). So one might logically wonder how tall he is in that more common position and how that compares to other large critters. Well, an adult male brown bear (on all fours) will stand over five high at the shoulder; the same height as the American bison or African hippo. The brown bear is a very respectable critter even when measured against these other very large animals - and he is a predator, which (of course) these other animals are not.

The color of the brown bears found on Kodiak is (surprise!) most often brown; a rich chocolate brown with lighter highlights across the prominent hump and shoulders. This varies widely and you'll sometimes run across very dark bears with long silver guard hairs giving them the "grizzled" appearance of bears found in the Rockies (the color pattern from which the name "grizzly" is drawn). There are also blond bears with bright yellow coats, very dark bears that look almost black and various combinations incorporating any of these color schemes.

The paws of a brown bear reflect (in a general way) the overall stature of a bear and allow us to use the tracks to gauge the size of the animal that made them. The front paws are shaped somewhat like that of a dog, that is of a roughly circular or oval shape, tipped with long claws. If you measure the width in inches and then mentally "add one" you get an estimate of the size of the bear (square foot of the hide) in *feet*. That is, front tracks eight inches in width indicate a nine-foot bear; nine-inch tracks would indicate a ten-foot bear, etc.

The rear tracks are much larger in size and shaped somewhat like a human foot. The rear paws of a large brownie are expansive enough that a large man can stand with both feet inside of such a track.

The claws of brown bears are nothing less than offensive weapons. If you examine the claws of a black bear, you will find they resemble those of a large dog, designed more for digging or gripping surfaces. In contrast, brown bear claws are more like those of the cat family; long curving sabers reaching out five to six inches or more in length on the larger males. I once measured a claw on a recently deceased bear that extended over six and a half inches on the outside curve.

Hunter trophy photos rarely give the viewer a good indication of how large these bears really are. It seems that as talented as some guides are in finding trophy bears, they rarely have a talent for photographing them. The typical trophy photo shows the hunter crouched some feet behind the bear so that the foreshortening effect supposedly makes the animal look larger. Unfortunately, that technique (as far as I am concerned) has the opposite effect. The eye recognizes the illusion and the viewer assumes the animal is actually much smaller than it really is.

Brown bear sows reach sexual maturity at five to seven years of age. They breed with males during late spring and early summer, though through one of those odd miracles of nature the actual implantation of the fertilized egg into the uterus will not occur until October/November, allowing the birth to take place in the den at the appropriate time. The sow will birth two or three cubs (rarely, as many as five) in the winter den between late January and March. Those cubs will stay with her for the next three years.

These new mothers and their progeny will be the last bears to depart the den come spring, as late as early June. Males and dry sows may depart their dens as early as late March. Occasionally (on temperate Kodiak at least), brown bears will not den at all, preferring to forage beaches for carrion thrown up in storms or to find winter-killed or weakened deer or other game. This seems to be particularly true of older males and may be somewhat weather dependent.

Brown bears in the wild commonly live up to 35 years. They are clever animals with long memories and one should keep that in mind when dealing with them. Those old bruins have learned quite a lot in their time. They are not easy to fool.

About those dens... Popular mythology brings to mind the picture of Yogi's roomy cave in a hillside. Perhaps some lucky bears do find such warm and cozy winter accommodations, but the average den is merely a hollow under a rock crevice or log that the animal will enlarge with a little digging. These are located at altitudes well above the winter snowline where the bear can count on a thick layer of the white stuff to seal and insulate the otherwise very inadequate winter bedroom. Bears do not "hibernate" in the strict biological sense of the term. That is, their body temperatures do not drop dramatically and they do not enter the comatose state of other true hibernators such as the raccoon or woodchuck. On the contrary, bears will maintain a fairly high body temperature and will even awaken periodically, sometimes even exiting the den for short periods during the winter. They are occasionally roused by activities outside the den and can react aggressively to such disturbances.

Late spring is a hungry time for bears. They have used up their winter fat supply and leave their dens to find a barren landscape devoid of any high calorie sources of food. The salmon will not arrive in substantial numbers until late June and the berries even later. On Kodiak, bears will rely heavily on an early plant known locally as "Pushky" (wild parsnip) for much of their sustenance during this period, as well as various grasses, bulbs and any carrion revealed by the retreating snowline. During this period bears will often be found on south facing slopes (where the first tender new growth of spring makes its earliest appearance), grazing like so many cattle. Low tides will often find them foraging beaches for clams and mussels.

Summer ushers in the mating season. Males and females in estrus will "hook up" for several weeks at a time, traveling together as a pair and breeding repeatedly. However (as described earlier) the actual implantation of the fertilized egg will not occur until much later. Other than sows with cubs, this is the only time when bears actually socialize with each other for any extended period of time. By late July, the partners will separate to begin the very important process of gathering enough fat to survive the winter.

Sows with cubs will savagely attack any boar (male bear) that approaches, due to the simple fact that the males will take any opportunity to snatch and eat cubs. At first thought, cannibalizing the young of your own species doesn't seem to make sense in strict Darwinian terms; however, biologists opine that boars kill the young under the reasonable assumption that they are the offspring of another male. A sow losing its cubs will become fertile again in the following year (instead of the two, three or four years that would normally ensue) increasing the odds that the killer will pass along *his* genetic material when estrus again ensues. At the very least, killing the cubs reduces competition for any offspring a boar might have with another sow. It is a cruel world – a world where the cold logic of genetic survival will disappoint tender human sensibilities.

June will bring the first salmon runs and the bears will begin to concentrate along rivers to claim fishing sites from previous years or challenge competitors for new ones. This happy period will last through September as waves of the various salmon species hit the rivers. The timing and order of the runs vary from stream to stream, but typically, you will see the very oily and desirable Reds (Sockeye) and Kings (Chinook) in June, followed by the Pinks (Humpies) and Dogs (Chum) in late July, then the Silver (Coho) in mid August. The food value of these various salmon is dependent on the amount of oil the flesh contains and therefore how much can be converted to the fat the bear requires to survive the winter. The oil content varies widely from the very numerous (and smaller) pink salmon which have a relatively low amount of the precious commodity, to the reds which contain so much that their dark crimson flesh has an oily sheen.

Bears are quite individual in their choice of fishing styles and preferred sites. Some will wait in the shallow water of gravel bars to pin exposed and vulnerable fish with their paws or grasp them in their jaws, while others will stand in deeper waters below rapids or waterfalls to grab fish from the dense schools held up in these places. A few photogenic bears have even learned to stand on the lips of small waterfalls to catch jumping fish in mid-air, much to the delight of wildlife photographers. There are almost as many fishing styles as there are bears and some are very successful at the game, while others are not. In fact, some bears are simply terrible at fishing and will struggle for each fish while others can catch one after another as quickly as they can eat them. Studies indicate that both the choice of sites and the style of fishing are passed down to cubs by the sow and that over the years, bears will learn refinements and improve their technique - more evidence of the "thinking" nature of bears. Regardless of their fishing style or success, this bonanza of rich oily salmon is a key event in the annual cycle. This feeding frenzy will determine the amount of fat the animal collects before another winter sets in.

Even in the salmon-rich Kodiak archipelago, there are locales where bears rely more heavily on other sources of food. I'm thinking here of small islands like Uganik and Raspberry which host only tiny streams with very limited runs of salmon, and those of the less-desirable species of pink salmon. Bears in such places will rely heavily on summer berries to sustain them, and a year with a poor crop can create havoc. The most common berry is a large red/black item known as a salmonberry. It resembles a raspberry in appearance, but is much larger and sweeter and has none of the tartness of that better-known fruit. These hardy shrubs are one of the most common plants encountered in the islands and the succulent berries can be harvested anywhere from exposed mountainsides just below the alpine tundra, down to dark spruce groves that never see direct sunlight.

A number of other berries are heavily utilized by bears. There are several species of blueberry (or huckleberry) to be found in wooded areas, as well as cranberries, lingonberries, crowberries, etc.

In the winter of 97/98, an unheard of cold snap descended on the region, destroying or freezing back generations of the rich berry growth that blankets the hillsides of Kodiak. Not surprisingly, the succeeding autumns of 98 and 99 saw an unprecedented number of bear attacks as hungry and stressed bears encountered deer hunters. Almost all of these incidents happened on the smaller islands where no sizable salmon runs offered a substitute for the lost berry crop.

By late September, the salmon runs have petered out. The streams still host a glut of spawned out and dying fish, but these specimens have used up most of the nutritional value they once contained. They are now just burned out husks of fish, their oily red flesh depleted to the pale white of a corpse, their skin blackened or covered with mildew. They collect in stretches of quiet water still feebly attempting to fight the current until inevitably; they turn belly up and sink to the bottom. Their nitrogen will return to the stream bed to fertilize the tiny flora that form the basis of the food chain throughout the stream - the food chain that next spring's crop of salmon will require when they burst from the eggs laid by the dying parents to begin the cycle anew.

Unconcerned with the delicate nuances of salmonid life cycles and stream ecology, the bears will begin to disperse from the rivers to find new sources of food. Late berries can be found through early October and young ten-der growth can still be found at the edge of the still-retreating mountain snow line, but as autumn progresses, bears find it increasingly difficult to locate quality sources of food.

Autumn finds the bears entering a biological cycle known as hyperphagia, a feeding frenzy when they are driven to exploit every source of food they can find to insure survival in the coming winter. Bears are restless and will cover large distances at this time of year, traveling to productive areas remembered from previous seasons or seeking out new regions entirely. They are also somewhat temperamental and more prone to aggressive behavior as winter approaches

At high elevation grows an interesting little ground-hugging fruit known locally as a "bearberry" but more widely known as "kinnikinnick" down in the lower 48. The leaves of this plant contain nicotine and it was a staple ingredient in the smoking mixtures of a number of Indian tribes throughout the mountain west. More importantly (for bears), the plant also produces a small nutritious berry which (I assume), is nicotine-free - one does not want to contemplate a thousand pound predator with a bad tobacco craving... The plant itself is almost invisible to the casual observer, growing along the ground amidst the more colorful lichens and mosses of the alpine tundra. Not realizing this, I was puzzled (on several occasions) to observe late season bears apparently "grazing" on what (to my eyes) was barren alpine tundra. It was not until much later that I actually looked closely, and running my fingers through this carpet of moss and lichens discovered an astonishing number of dull red berries threaded throughout the more eye-catching growth around them. The berries are rather tasteless to the human palate, but the bears don't seem to care. When the salmon and the sweeter berries of the low elevations are long gone, the bruins can still eke out an existence in these invisible berry patches on the heights.

Another (and much richer) source of nutrition for the hungry and opportunistic fall bears is cleaning up after human deer and elk hunters. Typically, a hunter will leave thirty or forty pounds of protein lying at the site of each kill; items like the hide, lungs, intestines and other internal organs, and bones containing rich marrow. This is simply waste material to a human, but bears are not nearly that fastidious and even the hide will be chewed up and converted to much-needed calories. These "gut piles" are a real bonanza for bears at this time of year and I can personally attest that many bears here have learned to follow hunters around and patiently wait for kills to clean up. On a number of occasions, I have witnessed bears following me around as I hunted, or found their tracks overlaying mine when retracing my steps. I have never found a gut pile out on the refuge that was more than 24 hours old. The bears generally scavenge these sites within hours (or even minutes) after the hunter departs.

I suspect that this is an important and largely unrecognized (by biologists) source of food for bears. This is a very hungry time and a critical one, coming as it does just prior to entering the den when any source of additional nutrition is valuable. Additionally, I would argue that this is an entirely natural phenomenon - bears have always scavenged the kills of other predators, including humans. In addition, despite arguments to the contrary by our Animal Rights friends, humans *are* a natural part of the environment!

Late fall and early winter will find bears moving to den sites. Sows with cubs will generally den first, followed by dry sows and then males.

These fall animals will have an entirely different appearance than the lean and rangy critters witnessed in spring and summer. Their weight has increased by 50% and the easy long-legged stride of the summer bear has been replaced by a ponderous ground-pounding march that radiates power and menace. The thin and dull summer coat has grown out until it is now six or eight inches in depth; an extravagant and multi-colored garment of great beauty and rich texture, with a glossy shine that catches the low autumn sun.

I have often lamented the fact that wildlife photographers tend to go for the easy shots of raggedy summer bears congregated on rivers instead of the same creatures, grown magnificent in their full autumn splendor. I suppose it is just more difficult (as well as dangerous) to get close to a fall bear with a camera. Whenever I pull up the image of a bear in my mind's eye, it is always that of a fall bear - a muscular giant standing before the red and gold backdrop of an Alaskan autumn.

Every year people in North America are killed by bears. Why does this happen and more importantly, how do we keep it from happening to ourselves?

There are no easy answers to the first question. They kill because they are bears and that is what bears sometimes do. It may view you as food, it may be protecting a food cache or cubs or perhaps be injured and thus "cranky." I think though, that most bear attacks are set off by nothing more than surprise. Bears sleep and drowse through much of the daylight hours when people are out and about, so it is not difficult to surprise one of these animals. On most occasions, they will simply awaken and flee. At other times, they will go into a threat display, puffing up and asserting dominance, but allowing you to edge away and de-escalate the situation. Occasionally, they will just wake up and kill you.

Chapter 3
Coming to Alaska

I first came to Alaska in the spring of 1990 with my wife Sandi and six-year-old daughter, Epi. We had been living in San Diego for the previous year, which is an attractive city to most people, but merely inflicted me with a growing sense of claustrophobia. The crowds, the traffic, the crime and the dirty yellow skies all combined to make me feel imprisoned and unhappy. I was in the Coast Guard then and began searching for some new (and cleaner) horizons.

I asked for a position in Alaska and was delighted when I got orders to the Coast Guard Cutter Storis, in Kodiak.

I had grown up in southern Michigan, in an area where a glance at the northern horizon would take in billowing clouds of industrial smoke. Even in such a place, I found peace whenever I explored the isolated stands of natural country that still escaped the urban sprawl. There were thousands of acres of old abandoned farmland growing back in a dense tangle of crabapple and wild grasses as well as large tracts of marshland- impossible to develop and offering habitat for plentiful waterfowl. In just a few places, there were still small groves of enormous oak and black walnut trees, which hinted at what the land, had once been. I loved to wander those places and I treasured every glimpse of the remaining wildlife. Occasionally, I would see a deer or a fox, which to my young imagination were every bit as majestic as a trophy moose or arctic wolf.

One summer at about eight or ten years of age, I encountered a black bear at our family campsite in Michigan; this was in the Porcupine

Mountains in the western Upper Peninsula. I was first out of bed and wandered out of the tent to head to the outhouse that served this little state campground and there on the trail ahead of me was a black bear. I still recall him quite clearly even after all these years. He was glossy and strong and I recall being surprised that even his snout was coal black instead of tawny like those pictured in the wildlife book I had at home. He didn't seem particularly interested in me, merely stepping off the trail into the berry bushes.

It was a different America then, and at about the age of twelve my dad bought me a light shotgun and taught me how to use it safely. After that, I would proudly bring home rabbits, pheasants and ducks, which my mom would prepare with great fanfare. In the summer, we would escape for short periods to the cool forests of northern Michigan to camp and catch trout from clean, clear rivers. All of this was in great contrast to the "other world" around me – the world of industrial pollution, crowds, traffic, dirt and noise. Somewhere in there, I began reading Jack London and dreaming of Alaska...

As a young man, I found myself working in a steel mill and then later as a railroad switchman hauling steel and ore to and from the mills around Detroit. My life might have been very different if (for a variety of reasons, including a failed marriage) I hadn't suddenly rebelled and left all that behind. I quit my job, threw some possessions in the trunk of my car and left to go looking, for *something...* A year later, I found myself in Florida enlisting in the Coast Guard.

The Coast Guard took me all over North America and the Caribbean, with various side trips to Europe and Asia. It was a vagabond life and one that I enjoyed immensely for many years until I finally found myself with a family and felt the need to establish some roots. I had no desire to go back to Michigan. My family there had long since dispersed. When I thought back to all the places the Coast Guard had taken me, I could not think of a place where I had really fit in. The east and west coasts were too crowded for my tastes, the south lacked good schools and was too damned hot. More and more I began to remember my boyhood dreams of Alaska.

Our ferry arrived in Kodiak on a sunny day at the end of March after an impossibly long and tedious winter journey up the Alaska Highway. In contrast to the gray winter landscape we had left behind on the Alaskan mainland, Kodiak was sparkling under a spring sun. The wild hillsides above the town were still brown and yellow, but the first tulips and crocuses were showing themselves in the gardens of homes along the channel. Eagles glided over us at (seemingly) arms length, while enormous Steller sea lions breached loudly in the clear green water below. Fishermen and idlers gave us friendly waves from the docks as we passed.

The small city itself was like a postcard, wrapped picturesquely around the foot of a mountain facing the sea. From our vantage in the channel, the town was dominated by an ancient and lovely Russian church with its blue ice-cream dome jauntily proclaiming a history far removed from the rest of white bread America.

I was charmed and delighted by this veritable avalanche of beauty. I had not expected anything quite like this, but suddenly realized that I did not ever want to leave this place. I looked at my daughter and could tell that she was as mesmerized by this magical scene as myself; her eyes lighting up at each new vista revealed by our slow passage up the channel. Epi laughed and pointed out each new and exciting thing that caught her young eyes, running from one side of the deck to the other to take in the eagles and wheeling gulls or the "water doggies" (sea lions) barking at us from the channel. Perhaps if we had arrived on one of those wet and blustery winter days that Kodiak is famous for, we would not have been charmed in the least, but we would still have grown to love this place in short order.

We often do not recognize the pivotal events in our lives until long after they occur. Who knows (at the time) that asking the girl in the gray dress (instead of the girl in red) for a dance will change both your lives? This event was very different and we all knew right then that this was not just going to be another three-year duty station, a place to be left behind when we grew bored. This was a sea change in our lives.

We were home.

That feeling has never really left me and even now after these many years, the sight of an eagle wheeling over my head or a low winter sun illuminating the mountains with a pink glow gives me that same heady sense of belonging that I first experienced on that sunny spring day.

There may be other places as beautiful (though I have not seen any), but Alaska, and in particular Kodiak, offers something else with even more value; in a word, it is the sense of *freedom* that beguiles and entices people like myself to places like this. This is a place where a twelve-year-old kid with a shotgun on the side of the road will elicit a smile and wave instead of a call to the SWAT team. While another person might complain of the lack of shopping, entertainment or cultural attractions, I would counter with the fact that we also lack the traffic, noise, pollution and crime that large concentrations of people create, along with the stress and misery that these things inflict on our psyche - a good trade from my perspective! You can live your life as an individual, rather than as another face in a crowd. One gains so much living in a place like this; not only the natural beauty and sense of independence and solitude, but the opportunity to experience actual adventure in an age when such a word no longer has any meaning in our lives. Where else can one experience adventure in a world that has become tamed, taxed, sanitized, regulated and equipped with guardrails?

I could not have articulated any of that in 1990 - I just knew that I had found a home, and that the path of my life had changed.

I was at sea for long periods on my Coast Guard duties, but took full advantage of any and all outdoor opportunities when I was at home. It had been years since I had hunted or fished, but I purchased equipment (often the wrong equipment) and jumped into the Alaskan lifestyle with both feet. When summer came, we picked berries and learned to make jams and jellies. We bought a smoker and put up enormous amounts of delicious salmon. Eventually, after a year's wait (to become an Alaska resident), I was able to begin hunting.

It was through deer hunting that I became well acquainted with bears. The deer on Kodiak are a smallish species known as the Sitka Black-tail, not quite as large as the whitetail and mule deer prevalent in the lower 48. These delicate deer are largely creatures of the mountains and a successful hunt generally begins with a steep climb. On Kodiak, you move abruptly from the tangled head-high vegetation of a marine climate to alpine tundra at about the 1000-foot level. Though deer can be found at all elevations, it is this alpine habitat that is preferred through the summer and fall as they follow up the retreating snow line to graze on new growth freed from winters grasp. Many deer will feed low at night and return to the alpine with the daylight, to escape predators and insects in the breezy heights. At any rate, for the hunter and hiker it is often not until they leave the tangled lowlands and stand perched on some overlook that observation allows them to appreciate just how numerous are the deer and other wildlife, and how invisible those creatures are when you are within the tangle of the low country with them. I've spent many a fascinating afternoon perched on some overlook and while ostensibly glassing for deer, becoming engrossed in all the other activities taking place below. You might see hunters wending their way through alder thickets while deer nimbly step aside or lay low until they pass - and you might see bears doing the same thing. Surely, such hunters must go home thinking they've crossed an area barren of wildlife, when in fact they've passed within rock throwing distance of many deer and perhaps a few bears as well.

Chapter 4
Bear Stories

I have had some very memorable close encounters with bears over the years. One of the first occurred on a sunny day in October at a place called Kizhuyak Bay. Autumn in Alaska is an especially beautiful time of year. At this latitude the late October sun (when you can see it through the mist) merely arcs across the southern horizon and gives the entire short day the feel and appearance of an eight hour sunset. This daylong sunset enhances the red end of the light spectrum and turns the end-less grassy mountainsides of Kodiak a brilliant yellow, broken by the crimson and orange of other growth. It was all new to me then and I remember thinking that it was like walking into a Van Gogh painting - a metaphor that returns to mind every year when the late October sun sinks to the horizon. My companion and I had run a skiff some miles from town and landed on a remote beach just after dawn, planning to hike up into a small valley that I had hunted earlier in the year. I think we were both struck by the beauty of the rare sunny day at this time of year. We certainly were not thinking of bears. The area was relatively open and treeless; a se-ries of grassy step-like knolls built into higher mountains further inland. The openness of the area (we thought) would allow us to see any bears from a distance and enable us to avoid them. We were headed up to a pleasant valley between two of those knolls, an area I had pre-viously hunted and found rich with deer.

The first large knoll was a steep grassy edifice perhaps six to eight hundred feet in height. We were both winded as we reached the crest and I recall that we stepped from shade into brilliant, blinding sunlight as we reached the top. Immediately, I became aware of a disturbance close at hand and looked to see an enormous bear not fifteen or twenty yards from us on our right. It was apparent that the bear had just jumped up from its bed overlooking the valley below, awakened by our presence and not in the least bit pleased about it.

It may not sound quite believable, but even in that situation fraught with menace; a part of my brain was contemplating the utterly compelling beauty of the scene that had unfolded. This was an enormous fall bear, a male, with his full winter supply of fat filling him out to epic proportions. Even with all that bulk, his muscles rippled beneath his glossy yellow fur, for this animal was of the relatively rare blond variety, his fur turned a luminous gold by the low red sun, a somewhat more brilliant gold than the grasses around him. He was standing in silhouette with the rays of the low sun behind him catching his long guard hairs and creating an odd halo effect. The scene had an odd sense of unreality – an impressionist painting come to life.

The bear was standing broadside to us, his head low, staring intently at *me*. I froze and began talking quietly to him: "Hello bear, nice bear!" The bear was so close - just a few yards away - that at first I didn't even consider pulling my rifle from where it hung on my shoulder. I was afraid any movement might startle the bear into action, and I fervently hoped that my companion behind me appreciated the situation in the same way. After a few seconds, the bear began walking, not directly away from us, but at an angle from right to left across our fronts. As he drew away a few yards (and while I was still speaking in gentle tones), I slowly pulled my rifle from my shoulder and raised it, trying to find his head in the scope – useless, the animal was so close that everything was just a blur! I had no intention of shooting unless there was no choice, and in any case was doubtful that my light deer rifle would even stop such an animal. The bear paused at my movement and suddenly made a loud "woof" - startling in the near silence of the moment. He followed that up by making loud clicking and popping noises with his teeth, snapping them together with an almost metallic sound while forcefully bobbing his head at each jaw click. We remained motionless.

The animal began to escalate his display, pounding the ground with his front paws while his guttural woofing and teeth clicking grew louder and more frequent. I could actually feel the vibration of the earth through my boots as he threw his enormous bulk into his ground pounding display. It was terrifying.

I knew little about bears beyond what I had read in various bear safety brochures put out by the State of Alaska, but I knew we were being challenged. If we ran, we would likely be viewed as prey and if we stood our ground, we were in effect, meeting his challenge. We had disturbed this mature old boar in his sunny napping spot, frightening him and forcing him to jump up and vacate his bed. Now he was seeing what we were made of, getting us back for the fright we had given him. This was when I first noted the expressiveness of a bear's eyes that I have alluded to earlier in this book.

When I first saw the animal, he had a startled and somewhat irritated expression – the same sort of look you see on a politicians face when the subject of campaign finance reform or term limits is broached. As the animal got his bearings and realized he had been awakened by a pair of puny bipeds, he began to change. His eyes narrowed and focused on me until they showed nothing but cold anger and barely contained fury! He was now a thousand pounds of junkyard dog with no restraining chain.

I was still covering the bear with my rifle as best I could, sighting along the plane of the barrel, shotgun style. Speaking quietly to my companion (who I knew was right behind me), I told him that I was going to start yelling and that I thought the bear would either charge us or leave when that happened and to be ready to shoot. In my mind's eye, I saw him a few yards behind me with his rifle leveled at the bear like my own, ready to do battle if the need arose. His rifle was a much heavier caliber and I was reassured somewhat by that knowledge. Later, I was to learn that my confidence was misplaced, my mind's eye lying to me.

I began yelling; "GET OUT! FUCK OFF! GIT!" at the top of my lungs, and the bear (somewhat to my surprise and relief) immediately closed for business and went on his way, pausing once at about fifty yards to woof back at me as if to say; "I was leaving anyway.", before disappearing over a rise.

This entire episode happened in less time than it takes to tell it - perhaps thirty seconds or even less. I turned to my heretofore boon companion to find him ashen faced and with his rifle still slung on his shoulder. He had frozen in that position when the bear first began his threat display and had been unable to move since then! Which (I suppose), is exactly what such a display is designed to accomplish... We found a place to sit down and catch our breath, and before long were laughing out loud at the entire situation. For my part, the episode had left me with a feeling of exhilaration, of having cheated death or mutilation and walked away the victor in a stone-age test of wills.

I had not realized until that time just how immense and powerful these bears were. I had seen them a number of times at a distance where the sheer scale of the country disguised their true nature. You merely saw a bear walking along the face of a mountain, or down a trail in the valley below you - interesting perhaps, but with none of the drama, power and "presence" that the animals generate at close range, when you realize how very large they are and meet their eyes to measure the intelligence and gravitas.

Sometimes you do not have to see the animal to feel that power. Once, while fishing the Karluk River, we heard the sound of a fawn crying in distress from the alder jungle across the river. This is a sound that most people would not associate with a deer, a series of high-pitched cries that can sharpen to an almost human scream in moments of great danger. We began glassing the thickets and soon spotted two bear cubs lying on a rise above and behind the alders. The distress cry was coming from much closer, in the tangle of alders perhaps fifty yards across the river from us. The sound rose to a series of piercing shrieks as the unseen drama reached its climax, and was then cut off as abruptly as a radio being unplugged. A few seconds later, we heard the "woof" of an adult bear from the same spot, and the two cubs jumped to their feet and hurried into the thicket to enjoy their meal. I was left with butterflies in my stomach at this sudden termination of life, all the more chilling because it remained unseen.

On another evening of that same float trip, we watched a large male bear walking along the river on the bank opposite our camp. It has always fascinated me to observe how such enormous animals can move so ghost-like through the almost impenetrable alder thickets that blanket much of Kodiak. However, on this occasion we were watching a very large bear with an attitude, one whose movements more closely resembled a bulldozer. We first spotted him in an open area along the bank popping his jaws in anger, his paws stomping the earth like a thousand pound toddler departing in a tantrum after being told he cannot watch TV with the older kids. The bear entered an alder thicket and we began to see the leaves shaking and hear the crack of wrist-thick branches being broken in the bear's fury as he continued on his path, obliterating everything before him. If we had not seen the bear enter the thicket, we might well have thought some large tracked vehicle was busting through. We were happy to have a river in between him and us, and I don't think either of us slept well that night.

That bear could have been angry about any number of things; perhaps an even larger bear had bested him out of a fishing spot or some angler had squirted him with pepper spray... Maybe he had a toothache?

We can't know the reason, but the fact that bears get into such moods is instructive in itself, a handy thing to remember when some "expert" tells you that a bear will act "like this" or "like that" in a given circumstance. In my opinion, bears can never be predicted because the options they may choose are dependent on the mood, health, past experiences or a host of other imponderables. These are thinking animals - predators that learn from experience, constantly modifying behavior to adapt to changing circumstances.

Lesser animals, prey animals, are heavily imprinted with instinctive behavior passed

down in their genes. One can pattern a ruminant from general observation of the species
and then apply that knowledge to an individual
animal with great success - ask any deer hunter.

A bear is not nearly as easy to predict. Each
bear is an entity unto itself with its own rules,
habits and behavior. Bears are individuals who
may choose one action one day, and quite another on the next. I do not mean to imply that
bears are completely free of the chains of instinct, only that they also rely heavily on their
intelligence and adaptability to overcome challenges, and (like humans) they can be moody
and unpredictable. That is a very valuable thing
to know.

A man living in a remote cabin not too far
from here learned that lesson in a rather painful fashion when a young bear took up resi-
dence near his home one spring. This was one
of those gangly three year olds recently kicked
loose from the sow. Such animals are vulnerable because they have not yet learned how to
care for themselves and often run into problems
from both humans and larger bears until they
learn how to make a living on their own. Most

of the problem bears one encounters on Kodiak are juvenile three or four year olds (ranging between two and four hundred pounds), driven by hunger to boldly approach camps, homes or village dumpsters. Anyway, this man had dealt with many bears in his time by driving them off and generally making their presence unwelcome around his home. This particular bear was so thin and hungry that the man took pity and allowed the bear to stay in the locale where it was apparently getting sustenance by clamming in the inviting tidal flat below his cabin. This went on for some weeks, the man going about his business at the cabin while the bear went on about his on the mud flat – a sort of nodding acquaintance between neighbors, if not a friendship.

One day as he walked near his cabin, the bear (for no apparent reason) simply charged him on sight, caught him, knocked him down and inflicted a painful mauling. The man survived by playing dead.

What had changed? Had the bear simply decided to assert its dominance as it recovered its strength? Had the animal laid some sort of territorial claim to the area? Had the man changed his cologne?

Another example of this unpredictability can be illustrated by an encounter of my own. I was deer hunting on Amook, a smallish island typical of much of the northwest coast of Kodiak in that it is densely covered with alder brush. Unlike other areas of Kodiak, there are no mountains on this small island high enough to allow one to escape the tangle by climbing into the alpine. Hunting in such an area is difficult at best because the limited visibility works heavily in favor of the deer. I had climbed up the slopes of a small steep hill to a relatively bald area near the top in order to gain a vantage point over the thicker tangle at lower elevations. I spent some time glassing the thickets for deer, but without success as it was late in the morning and the deer had already bedded down for the day. I had with me a deer call of the type known as a "fawn bleater." These types of calls work by imitating a fawn in distress, which at times will call in a curious deer, but in most cases merely causes them to stand and look, revealing themselves to the hunter who can then plan a stalk to their location.

Of course, imitating "prey in distress" with such a call is a double-edged sword in bear country and should only be attempted in areas of high visibility. Unwisely (as it turned out), I decided to use the call, reasoning that from my fairly high vantage I could easily see any bears coming and take steps to vacate the area well before they arrived. I blew a short series of calls and sat back to glass the thickets for movement. After a short wait, I heard the faint noise of an animal's approach through the dry brush *behind* me, coming down an alder choked ravine which (apparently) terminated at the top of the hill only a hundred or so yards above. This little ravine contained the only thick brush for some distance around me. I thought about bears for a moment, but the sounds were so faint and the shallow ravine so entangled that I reasoned that only a deer could be making those sounds - surely no bear could be making its way through that dry jungle with such delicacy. I took a few steps to the edge of the ravine and because it was impossibly thick and close, I laid down my scoped rifle, drew a .45 (1911) pistol and waited - knowing that I would not see the deer until it was just a few yards away.

Within a few moments I saw movement, readied my pistol and... was suddenly facing a sow bear with two very young cubs a scant five yards away from my wavering (and quite inadequate) pistol.

I spoke gently; "Hello bear, nice bear, good bear!"

She merely looked at me curiously and then with an air of faint irritation turned around and began herding her cubs slowly back up the ravine. This episode may sound anti-climactic, but it is another illustration of the animal's unpredictability. All of the elements here - a sow in predator mode, with cubs, in a surprise close-range encounter with a human add up into the formulaic equation of the archetypical American bear mauling tale. Yet, this sow disappoints us by reacting with almost complete equanimity in the situation, dismissing the human as just one more annoyance among many that a mother has to deal with.

Nice bear, good bear!

One glorious summer day I went out to Afognak Island with a friend to run some set nets. These are gill nets that you run out perpendicular from shore to intercept salmon as they return to their streams. Ideally, you want to set your net off a point or in a narrow spot in a bay where the migrating salmon tend to be especially thick as they pass the obstruction, thus our long trip to this favored bay on Afognak, a couple of hours away by skiff.

We set a couple of nets about a half mile apart and we'd run along one net detaching all the salmon (Silvers), take them ashore, filet and pack them and then run to the other and do the same. We were having a great morning and must have had 100 or 120 fish by the time the tide changed and the net began coming up nearly empty. Rather than go home, we decided to leave the nets to soak for a few hours and run to the river mouth some way up the bay to see if we couldn't catch some fish on our rods. We had to hike a mile or so from where we could safely land the skiff. It was one of those warm, still days when you can hear the humming of mosquitoes in the brush and the jump of a fish hundreds of yards away would startle you with the abrupt slap.

Oddly, we began to hear snoring coming from the brush above the beach ahead of us and so we silently stalked in as close as we dared to find a big dark bear lying in the grass sound asleep, obviously torpid after a morning of salmon gluttony! For some reason, this sight struck both of us as extremely funny, so much so that we had to bite our lips to keep from laughing aloud. This grand old bear was lying amid a cloud of insects snoring and burping away like an obese alcoholic, yet we both knew that if we made any noise and woke him up, he would not find the situation nearly as funny as we did. I had a mental image of putting shaving cream on his paw and tickling his face. What a hilarious video that would make... right up until the screaming began. Somehow, we managed to back out of there without busting out with laughter and waking him.

I always remember that gluttonous bear when people express doubt that a bear can be surprised by a hiker or fisherman.

In Alaska (and especially in places like Kodiak), it is considered sound wisdom to take a firearm (or pepper spray), whenever you go into the bush for any reason. People here accept this in the same fashion that people elsewhere do the wearing of seatbelts. The odds are long in favor of not needing a particular safety device on a given day, but safety is good to practice for its own sake.

Doctor Rosenblatt (not his real name) was a cranky and opinionated curmudgeon with bad eyesight, worse hearing and all the social graces of a Marine drill instructor with a cheap whiskey hangover. He was just one of those sour personalities alienated in other places but at home in Alaska where odd people are commonplace and eccentricity accepted and encouraged. His face was dominated by a pair of glaring eyes enlarged by a pair of horn-rimmed bifocals and topped with bushy gray eyebrows that began the day looking like sleepy porcupines, but gradually turned into enraged wolverines as he fueled himself with numerous cups of black coffee. This visage was divided in half by a beak as sharp as the prow of a dreadnought, streaked with rusty red veins.

He was difficult to deal with at first, but after a period of trading barbs with this prickly old Captain, I began to recognize things that were not apparent at first. He usually delivered his bluster with a faint twinkle in his eye and could often be found in his office after hours or on weekends poring over patient's charts when no one else was around. He would call his patients at home to check on their progress or to urge compliance with his latest regimen, something I never saw any of the other physicians do. He practiced medicine with hard work and a lifetime of experience and we were all happy he somehow landed in Kodiak, even though he thought bedside manner was a big house in England. Apparently, such niceties had not been part of the curriculum in whatever medieval university had awarded him a degree in days of yore.

There was only one person who could calm his irascible temper. At that time, we had a very shapely female lab technician whose stern was often favorably compared to a pair of freshly caught salmon squirming around in a scoop net. This phenomenon was especially evident when she bent low over her equipment in her freshly pressed scrubs, and even the doc was in the habit of visiting the lab to ask for obscure tests just to take in this awesome sight. The panorama would tame his brows into a pair of sleek and purring otters for a time. Eventually, he would wander off to jolt himself with another cup of coffee, which in due course would herald the return of the rabid wolverines. When he was in an especially bad mood and jabbering at the junior enlisted people, I would throw aside my paperwork and tell him "those labs" he was waiting for were ready. Frequently there would actually be a lab result waiting for him when he got there. If not, he'd hang around there for awhile anyway and return distracted, forgetting whatever had irritated him before he left.

In reality, the doctor was a painfully shy, lonely professional who expected others to maintain the same high standards as he did, and thus was always disappointed and cranky about it. His poor hearing was probably the real reason his acidic commentary was delivered loud enough to scare salmon back to salt water.

Among his many failings, the good doctor (and he really *was* a very good doctor) was the worst angler to ever set foot in Alaska. On summer evenings, you could find him just outside of town at the heavily fished Buskin River. He would flog that stream to a froth with a variety of sure-fire flies in an attempt to catch the elusive and prized Silver Salmon – an enterprise doomed from the start by his lack of patience and even more so by his foghorn voice that scattered schools of fish as effectively as a hand grenade. I don't think doc could have caught a salmon with a hand grenade; he just did not have the feel for it. Rosenblatt was to salmon fishing as Chico Marx was to the Elizabethan Theater.

Kodiak Silvers (or Coho) are unusual in that they weigh nearly twice as much as the same species found elsewhere. A Coho in mainland Alaska or the Pacific Northwest might weigh seven pounds while the same article in Kodiak might go twice that, with an occasional bruiser breaking the twenty-pound mark. Most anglers agree that pound for pound the Silver is the most powerful of the five Pacific Salmon species. Hooking a Kodiak silver in a rushing stream is an unforgettable event - an event that eluded and frustrated Rosenblatt.

A multi-tasking individual, he not only managed to frighten fish for dozens of yards around, but would also infuriate every fisherman within earshot by loudly complaining whenever someone else caught a fish or threw a lure anywhere near what he considered "his water." He would decry anyone who used roe as an "egg-dunking moron" and berate hapless tourists as "amateurs" advising them to go home and catch carp in Iowa. To Rosenblatt, all tourists were Iowans for some reason.

You would think a man with as much piscatorial hubris as Rosenblatt would have a freezer full of salmon filets, but he rarely caught anything. Now, he often *claimed* to catch fish and his veracity on the subject was unquestioned by those who did not know him... folks from Iowa mainly.

To be fair, it is often difficult to catch fish in the Buskin. The river is just outside town and heavily fished by the locals. The salmon there tend to be nervous and wary after threading the gauntlet of so many lures. Against my better judgment, I asked the doc if he would like to accompany me on a fishing trip to the Saltery River. The Saltery is a remote stream that can only be accessed by four-wheel drive after a rugged journey of some 15 miles along questionable trails. I reasoned that in waters teeming with unwary salmon, even Rosenblatt might catch a fish or two. To my surprise (and later to my regret), he eagerly agreed to go. Over the next few days, he grilled me incessantly about every detail; my vehicle, trail conditions, fishing regulations, bears and finally; guns.

One of his strongly held opinions was that guns were the "Tools Of Morons" - unless they were *his* guns and used for very specific purposes, like shooting deer (or shooting *at* deer), since the doc was a notoriously poor shot and brought home less deer than fish. Other than that, he had little use for guns and anyone who disagreed was a "Neanderthal" with "Manhood Issues."

Knowing the river was prime bear country, I had planned to toss a .44 in my backpack as "bear insurance" without telling the doc. However, at best a handgun is of questionable utility against an animal the size of a Kodiak bear and not wanting to argue with the doc all day (should he detect the weapon), I rejected the idea. I made a mental note to bring a can of pepper spray as a bear deterrent, but I did not have any at home and failed in the course of the week to buy any. I wasn't too worried, as no rational bear would care to eat anyone as sour as Rosenblatt.

The anticipated day dawned warm and sunny, perhaps one of the last beautiful summer days that year. In those days, I had a wonderful female wolf-hybrid named George. She was a great companion in the backcountry, a "dog" that could sense animals at great distance and was quick to warn me of bears. She also had a few bad habits; most notably a tendency to find any putrefying matter within extreme olfactory range, then roll around in it. This made return vehicle journeys home a terrible trial for any-one that did not enjoy the scent of rotting carri-on. I opted to take her along anyway, reasoning that her bear awareness outweighed any sensory outrage she might inflict on such a warm day when we would have all the windows rolled down.

The drive there was somewhat uneventful. There had been heavy rains earlier in the week and a few of the stream crossings were chancy but we trudged through without any problems until we reached a stretch of trail about a mile from our intended fishing site. At this point, we found the trail blocked by an enormous watery expanse which when examined revealed a very soft bottom of deep gelatinous mud. A fresh beaver dam just off to the right explained our trail's sudden end. Having your expensive SUV stuck axle deep in mud a dozen of miles from the nearest road is a bad business and I did not want to tear up the landscape (or the vehicle) by forcing our way through the brushy terrain surrounding the new pond. We parked and continued on foot loaded down with packs and fishing gear. We had not gone very far when George began to focus on the ground and bristle up to let me know she'd caught the scent of bear. That fact would have been apparent to us in short order anyway, since the track we were following was covered by huge prints from many different bears and generously strewn with large piles of scat. Enough that Rosenblatt suggested we return for the SUV. We did not do that, but in hindsight, it may not have been such a bad idea.

The bear sign was making the doc very uncomfortable. Until that moment, the whole subject of bears had been entirely abstract to him. He had never encountered any bears while fishing the Buskin or practicing medicine in any of the other shabby coastal towns the service had sent him. The big loveable fur-balls were relatively scarce near town and the proximity to humans made them largely nocturnal and thus rarely seen. Now however, he was observing bear tracks as large as dinner plates, and we were following them to their termination point on the river ahead where we would (in effect), compete with the owners of those tracks for food. We were walking along a narrow four-wheeler track enclosed within alders and cottonwoods until it became more of a tunnel than a trail. The doc was beaded with sweat and I heard a gulp and something that might have been Yiddish, or perhaps simply the sound a man makes when he is dying inside. He had stepped in a pile of bear scat the size of a pizza but not so thin and far more aromatic.

The Doc stopped dead at this and I paused beside him. He looked up from his foot and glared at me from beneath bushy gray brows, then straightened (and assuming his most irritatingly pedantic manner), fired an unexpected broadside: "Did you have the sense to bring that damned magnum revolver?"

He knew the answer as well as I since he was the reason I left it at home. I was caught flat-footed by his accusatory manner and the un-predicted opening of hostilities. I considered steaming for shelter, firing a light volley of reason and logic like smoke-shells to cover my escape - a weak and paltry tactic that doc would seize upon in an instant and shred to bits. Instead, I tried blame-shifting back at him; "It was *you* who asked me not to bring it! In fact, I think your exact words were; 'I don't want to be alone in the woods with any man toting a three pound stainless steel phallus!' Do you recall that conversation?"

"For once you pay attention to my advice? I thought you'd hide it in your rucksack no matter what I said!"

Clever fellow, I had considered doing that very thing... As I feared, logic bounced off the doc's rusty hull without even scratching the paint. I would need heavier artillery if I wanted to sink HMS Rosenblatt, something that could turn his growing paranoia to my advantage.

I began with a ranging shot; opening with the simple observation that "Brown bears are difficult to kill with a lousy handgun and I'm afraid if I shot one it would just piss him off. Better to use you as a decoy while I run for help."

He did not laugh. His head began to swivel about slowly peering into the thicket for the unsanitary bears. This change of tack made him discard any rant he was planning to deliver. Doc would have to reformulate the script for an entirely different rant, along new and unexpected lines. Surely, he was up to the challenge!

I had returned fire and had him bracketed, but did not quite know whether to turn to Port or Starboard to evade his next salvo. To buy time and bring the debate back to familiar ground, he shot back with "If not for bears, what possible reason can you have for owning that ridiculous hand-cannon, anyway?"

I had heard this all before and immediately recognized the foundation of one of his textbook rants on firearms. He would soon steer the conversation around to his own strange brand of psychoanalysis and I would have to endure a pseudo-Freudian examination of my many and various 'manhood issues' as evidenced by my choice of firearms. He knew everything, being an MD after all.

I was ahead of him this time and evaded his little snare by saying: "A bear can only catch the slowest runner, and I'm not very fast." I now had him and was adjusting my heavy guns to begin firing for effect.

He was rendered nearly speechless by the unexpected reply, his bushy eyebrows shot up and began a staccato vibration not unlike a pair of mating wolverines: "What in the hell does that mean?"

"It means that if a bear is chasing me, I can always shoot my fishing partner in the foot; it's an old Indian trick my neighbor Hank taught me..."

He fell silent for some moments, his eyes goggling widely behind his bifocals. His bushy brows fluttered to a halt. The mating wolverines were now in a post-coital cuddle as he considered and discarded various salty replies. The deck crew on battleship M.D. was beginning to hoist out the lifeboats before he finally got very pithy and said "That's not real funny, Keith."

Then his brown eyes lit up and the wolverines began a little slap and tickle action as a new thought crossed his mind. He turned to me in triumph and pointing a finger at my chest, launched a surprise torpedo: "Yes, but did you bring any pepper spray?" He was sporting a wicked little grin, certain his latest torpedo would find its way right up my stern! He was mentally rubbing his hands with glee at the thought of machine-gunning my lifeboat after the ship went tits up. The wolverines were now doing something vaguely obscene above his bi-focals.

"Nope, I don't have any pepper spray either, sorry." The old boy had me, what else could I say? I began mentally exploring whether it would be nobler to go down standing at the helm while bravely saluting the colors, or retire to my cabin and stick a Luger in my mouth.

His voice rose in triumph as he fully realized the ramifications of this new (and somewhat valid) rant-building opportunity! He closed in to point blank range to finish me off with a sarcastic salvo that would gut me entirely and send me to the bottom. He skewered me with his eyes and brayed out with his foghorn voice: "Don't you have any freaking idea how SERIOUS this situation is? Only a complete FUCKING MORON would come out here to Grizzly-Central without pepper spray!" There was silence.

"You got any?" I managed to get that out just as he was taking a deep breath to follow up his tirade of venom.

The Doc had opened his hatch just wide enough for me to get in a lucky shot. I heard the clang as my projectile rattled its way down into his boiler room. The steerage passengers broke through the cordon of deckhands and began swarming the lifeboats. Rosenblatt's mouth opened momentarily then snapped shut as he reconsidered the actual number of morons present. A rumbling blast emanated from the engine room and he began to list and slide under the waves.

He tried to rally the crew once more, raising a finger in the air at a 45-degree angle, began to speak and then paused, deflated. The wolverines collapsed as if head shot. He sighed dejectedly and turned to walk up the trail, his head rotating side to side as if on ball bearings, watching out for any bears lurking in the bushes.

I knew there were no bears in our vicinity because Georgie girl was making short circuits around and ahead of us and would warn us. She would bristle at the scent on the trail, but only in a general way as if the tracks were from the previous night or yesterday.

I wasn't about to tell any of this to the doctor and spoil my fun. If a bear ate me for lunch, he would have a happy meal.

I was not very concerned because I had fished there many times before and knew the river got a fair amount of human traffic, thus the bears were relatively shy and "trained" in consequence. In addition, there was a lodge up the river a ways and the guides were in the habit of squirting pepper spray at any bear they could find – it made for a good show and a good tip from grateful clients whose life had been "saved" by the selfless courage of these wilderness heroes.

The trail roughly paralleled the river, which was now perhaps a quarter mile to our left. When we reached the stretch adjacent to my favorite fishing hole, we turned off on a smaller path that led through some dense alders and cottonwoods down to the river. At this point George did something odd – she zeroed in on a small area of grass and circled it bristling and making small growling noises. After a few moments, she squatted there and marked the spot in the time-honored way of all canines then went on her way, looking quite pleased with herself. I noticed this but did not realize it had any significance until later that day.

This smaller trail was heavily covered in bear tracks and scat but we got to the river in short order and began a great day of fishing, a truly wonderful day for Rosenblatt. It was late in the season and the river was black with fish. Recent rains had boogered up the trail and discouraged locals from coming through, so the undisturbed fish were eager to throw themselves on our hooks. This dearth of recent human activity was also no doubt responsible for the increase in bear traffic that was clearly in evidence everywhere around us. The whole area stank of discarded fish parts; the stream banks were littered with bones and broken down by the passage of all the bears. I had never seen evidence of so much bear activity along this river.

I showed him how to crimp down the barbs on lures and we were able to catch and release the fish unhurt, only keeping the ones that were injured in some way. Those went into an ice chest we had carried down for that purpose.

The doctor had forgotten his worries and was in the moment; finally finding that Alaska fishing experience he had dreamed about for so long, but which eluded him until this glorious September day.

I would re-ignite his fear every occasionally by suddenly staring into the bushes and saying: "Did you hear that?" just to keep him from getting too happy and upsetting the natural balance of his gloomy personality. Happiness might be to Rosenblatt as sunlight was to a vampire and I didn't want to see all that happy overcome him and make him burst into flames, since we already had more fish in the cooler than I could legally take on my fishing license alone.

While we fished, George took off on little adventures of the canine variety. Occasionally, I'd see her hopping wolf-like in the grass, catching and eating live mice (disgusting habit) or swimming across the river above or below us, always returning after a few minutes to check in. In Alaska, the day can linger long even in September, but eventually the shadows began to lengthen and we had to terminate our fun before we faced a dark trail homeward. While the Doc caught 'one last fish', I busied myself packing up our gear and filleting our catch. George suddenly appeared at my side bristling with excitement, nudging my legs and glaring up the river to alert me to the presence of a bear. Try as I might, I could not really catch sight of any animal in the dark thicket that she indicated. I thought there was some movement behind the screen of brush, but in the growing darkness, I was unsure. I didn't need to see anything to be convinced, since I implicitly trusted her sharp senses. Evening was coming and the bears wanted their fishing hole back.

"What's that wolf of yours all excited about?"

"She sees something up there in the thick stuff."

"For the sake of conversation, could this be maybe a bear?"

"It *is* a bear - you ready to go?"

The sun was setting on that long dark trail through the undergrowth. We stashed the last gear in our packs and carrying the heavy ice chest full of fish between us, started off up the trail towards the SUV. George stayed so close that I kept bumping her with my legs, which caused me to stumble with my heavy, awkward load. She was bristled up and making throaty growls, her attention riveted to the upstream side of the trail where she had originally detected danger.

I began to get the impression that a bear was pacing us, just out of sight in the brush to our left and the farther we went and the darker it got, the larger that bear became.

That was almost certainly not the case. Doubtless, one or more bears were merely lying up in that large thicket patiently waiting for us to leave after having come down for an evening feed to find us monopolizing their fishing spot. At least, I can state that with some assurance today from the safety and comfort of my warm home! However, at the time I was convinced we were being stalked; that a ton of slavering nightmare from the Pleistocene was staring at the back of my neck, waiting for the opportunity to pounce on me. Rosenblatt was not helping the situation, keeping up a steady stream of acidic complaints and commentary on the state of my mental health for bringing us to this pass. Didn't I know there were bears out here? Why hadn't we left earlier? Didn't I realize it was getting dark? Why hadn't I brought a gun?

His commentary suddenly ceased, as did his grasp of the ice chest, which fell hard against my ankle.

He was staring down the trail with wide eyes, the wolverines scrambling halfway up his forehead in fear. I followed his gaze to see that the trees and brush ahead looked as if a tornado had touched down. Broken branches littered the area, the white scars on the scrubby trees revealing where they had been torn loose. Fresh dirt and tufts of grass lay scattered around and I suddenly realized that a section of grassy turf the size of a dinner table had been ripped from the earth and torn to pieces.

This was the fork where we had turned off the main trail that morning. The bed of turf, which had been so violently removed, was the very place George had left her urinary calling card. Canines and bears are distant relatives and no doubt, her calling card had been rejected, with extreme prejudice. I think the wolf understood the message because she was no longer bristling with threat, but hanging behind me, her tail drooping between her legs.

It was an amazing scene. While we had blithely enjoyed our afternoon, some bear had gone on a rampage here, ripping up trees, brush and the earth itself to protest our presence. Talk about intolerance! We were standing there in the growing darkness with forty or fifty pounds of fresh bloody fish in our hands, a mile from the car and safety.

We covered that remaining distance in record time despite the darkness and the load we carried. Every step of the way, while one ear was inflicted with the peppery commentary of my companion, the other was keenly picking up every rustling leaf, every flitting bird and it all sounded like the stealthy stalk of an angry bear.

I never went into grizzly country again without an appropriate firearm or a can of pepper spray, and I never went fishing with Rosenblatt again either, but I did notice that the wolverines above his bifocals were more subdued in my presence after that. We were friends.

Two acquaintances chartered a plane into the western Brooks Range for a combination moose/caribou hunt a few years ago. This is up in northern Alaska - the true arctic; a country of tundra and barren slopes with a few stunted forests along the river bottoms. They had hunted this area before and found that while there were relatively few bears, these mountain grizzlies seemed to be unusually aggressive compared to the more easy-going bears of Kodiak, with which they were better acquainted. In light of this, they both bought bear tags prior to the trip; not with any intention of hunting these smaller inland bears, but merely to forestall any problems if they were forced to shoot one. In hindsight, that precaution proved to be very wise. I won't use their names, but these men were also medical professionals, a doctor and a dentist.

As described to me, they were camped on the shores of a small lake with high barren slopes rising around them. This afforded them the opportunity to sit near camp and glass an enormous amount of country to locate game animals. This area was also a sort of natural funnel leading down from the mountains, a pass that animals seasonally traversed to move out of the high country ahead of the approaching winter. It was an ideal situation for a hunt and they were seeing many game animals; so many that they could afford to be quite selective in looking for mature old bull caribou and moose - animals approaching the end of their natural lives.

They were also seeing a number of bears. They saw several small and rangy mountain grizzlies moving restlessly along the slopes, stopping to graze at the sparse berry patches they encountered. One day while they were in camp following lunch, a bear approached. The dentist was down at the lake washing up when he looked back to see a light blond grizzly walking into camp. His rifle was up near the tents, closer to the bear than to himself. His companion (the doctor), was sitting in the doorway of a tent fiddling with his rifle (a 7mm Remington Magnum), perhaps cleaning it or making some small adjustment. The bear was behind him, beyond the tent, which blocked his view of the animal and its approach. The dentist shouted a warning and the doctor rose with his rifle and not realizing how close the animal was, paused to zip the tent flap closed. He then began backing down towards the lake where his companion stood, all the time keeping his rifle at the ready.

At this moment, the bear stepped around the edge of the tent and caught sight of the doctor, no more than eight or ten yards away. I think they were both caught by surprise – the doctor had assumed the animal was some distance away rather than just on the opposite side of the tent from him. At the instant, the bear caught sight of the standing man, it charged. There were no growls, no posturing or warning whatsoever. The animal went from curious examination of some odd human artifacts it had come across, to a deadly attack in a split second! The physician was caught by surprise, but ready - his rifle against his shoulder, the safety off. He fired and the shot caught the sprinting bear in the shoulder. The angry animal went down and skidded to the man's feet, still alive, and already beginning to rise as the doctor jacked another shell into the chamber. He fired again, and a third time before the animal was dead.

Both of these men were considerably shaken by the incident - in particular, by the abruptness of the event and the fact that there was no pre-cipitating factor to account for it in terms they could readily understand. The bear had simply seen a human and charged. As we will see later, this is quite typical of grizzly attacks.

That bear was skinned and proved to have a hide measurement of only six feet. There was little fat on the bear and the hide was badly scarred from old injuries, its teeth worn down to nubs. A molar was later extracted and exam-ined by the state (as is required for bears tak-en in Alaska) and the bear was found to be 29 years old - a very advanced age for a bear up in the arctic. This elderly fellow was (without a doubt) having a difficult time making a living in this rough and barren landscape. Perhaps that explains his unfriendly disposition...

Ranching is a risky business anywhere, but on Kodiak, it is an extreme proposition that would be impossible if not heavily supported with taxpayer dollars. Leaving that distasteful aspect aside, a number of people have run cattle on the northeast corner of the island, with varying degrees of (heavily subsidized) success. A few years ago, a Kodiak rancher began missing cattle. At that time, most of the cattle around were of a Scottish Highland breed - small, tough animals that seemed well suited to the area. I suspect the missing cattle were of that variety, but memory fails to dredge up the exact details. At any rate, some state officials went out with the rancher and after an extensive search found seven dead cattle in a pond. Due to the varying degree of decomposition in each carcass, it appeared that they had been killed on seven successive nights. Each animal had been disemboweled and had its internal organs eaten, then been dragged over and deposited in the pond. One of the officials surmised that the bear was perhaps an elderly animal with bad teeth that liked soft meat, so had dined on the organs and then deposited the cattle in the pond to soften up. I am not so sure, I lean to the theory that the animal was just an epicure who had been brought up on the gut piles of deer hunters. The bear in question was never found (to my knowledge), so the question of whether it was elderly bear or a gourmet will never be answered.

One might wonder how a bear can kill an 800 or 1000-pound cow without being gored in the process. Some fifteen years ago, I was treated to some grainy 8mm film of a bear killing a cow. The footage was taken not far from town at Middle Bay back in the 1950's and showed a bear chasing what appeared to be a Hereford, through tall grass. The bear quickly overtook the cow and with one bone-crushing blow of a paw, broke its neck. The bears triumph only lasted a moment, because he was rapidly shot down by someone off camera. The story was that this bear had been preying on cattle in the area and a local photographer had gone out to shoot film of the ensuing hunt. The bear was spotted from a car and the photographers delay in getting his camera set up cost the rancher a cow when the rifleman held his fire for the money shot. I am sure in those pre-FDA days, nobody cared much that the cow had suffered an untimely demise and no doubt, the steaks and hamburger were just as tasty.

One of the more interesting encounters I had with a bear took place on the main island of Kodiak not far from where my mauling took place a few years later. It was another of those late season deer hunts where one is more concerned about the elements than grizzly bears, and indeed, this mid-December hunt had been plagued with bad weather that kept us near camp most of the time. We endured several days of wet snow and rain with only intermittent breaks in the clouds. To make matters worse, we were on the north side of a mountainous peninsula that blocked the low sun of December from shining on our miserable camp, even when the scudding clouds allowed an occasional appearance of that distant orb.

Things changed when we awoke one morning to find a relatively clear sky and a gusty northwest wind announcing a high-pressure front that (we knew from experience) would give us several days of clear and cold weather. Days are short at that time of year and we wasted no time hiking up onto the spine of the peninsula where the deer would be found. It wasn't long before we spotted several dozen deer scattered across a snowy mountainside on the far side of a narrow canyon. In no time, at all we edged our way through the brush until we were opposite them, picked out a couple of young (and tender) bucks and fired. My partners deer dropped in its tracks, and so did mine... but then slid several hundred yards down the hill (dead) to disappear into the alder jungle at the bottom of the ravine.

We were unable to cross at that point because of the near vertical walls on our side of the canyon. We hiked along the lip for a while until we found a place to get across, whereupon we separated, my partner climbing the opposite wall while I fought my way through the dense brush on the floor of the ravine to get to the point where my deer had landed. This spot was perhaps a quarter mile down the ravine and I had no trouble finding the young buck because his "landing zone" was clearly defined by the skid mark down the snowy hill on my right. There he was, caught in the brush on the wall of the ravine; a hundred pounds of toothsome young venison waiting to be removed from the bone and carried out in my frame pack.

I leaned my rifle against a small tree and dragged the deer a few yards onto some level ground to facilitate the de-boning process. I dropped my pack, dug out my knife and had just knelt beside the deer when I heard a slight noise a few yards down the ravine (in the direction opposite my approach). My first thought was that this was another deer, and I wasn't interested since a full load of venison was already lying at my feet That notion was dispelled almost immediately as the unmistakable shape of a bear appeared in the alders less than twenty feet away. He (or perhaps she...) was a medium sized specimen of the common dark brown color. The animal paused momentarily to look at me and then began to approach. There were no growls or threatening mannerisms of any kind, the animal (apparently) was just following its nose to the source of the blood smell and my presence was not going to deter him in the least.

I had left my rifle some yards away when I had begun dragging the deer, and now the bear, the rifle and I, made up the three points of a triangle. The other significant object in that triangle was the deer and it did not take a genius to figure out that this was the object of the bear's desire. I quietly began to withdraw towards the wall of the ravine in the general direction of my rifle, some ten yards away. I was clutching a small skinning knife in my hand (a pitiful excuse for a weapon), and muttering my now familiar: "Nice bear, good bear!" Fortunately, the bear showed almost no interest in me, merely glancing my way once or twice as it calmly approached the deer. It nuzzled the carcass momentarily and then picked it up by the base of the neck and walked away in the direction it had come, carrying the deer with no more trouble than a beagle with a rabbit.

The grizzly had come and gone before I had covered half the distance to my rifle.

I was stunned by what had just happened! In the immediate aftermath, the entire episode did not seem real and I actually thought (for a moment), that I'd had some sort of hallucination, but clearly, there were the bear tracks in the snow and the deer *was* gone... I suddenly felt claustrophobic and frightened in the enclosed and shadowy floor of this deep canyon. My heart began beating a tattoo that the drummer from Metallica would envy. I was hyperventilating and light-headed, and I wanted to get up into the sunlight and safety of the open hillside RIGHT NOW! I grabbed my gear and rifle and scrambled up the very same hill I had earlier adjudged too steep to descend. I climbed straight up to the point from which I had initially taken my shot across the canyon.

It was not until I got there and found myself in the sun again that I began to decompress and put things in context. Upon reflection, I realized that this bear had not menaced me in any way. It had merely smelled a meal and taken it, paying me no more attention than if I had been a raven pecking at the carcass.

On the plus side, I had not yet clipped my tag for the taking of that deer. I am sure a strict interpretation of the law would find me guilty of some violation since I shot another deer with that tag on the following morning. Those tags are for feeding *my* family rather than the local wildlife and I will apologize on the day some grizzly brings me a deer to replace the one I lost.

A very similar episode happened a few years later on another part of the island, but by then I had learned to take these episodes with some equanimity. This was a late November hunt with quite a bit of wet snow. Almost from the first, we noted that a very large bear was following us around as evidenced by the tracks overlaying ours whenever we returned to the forest service cabin we had rented on a remote beach. This went on for several days and we noted that he was cleaning up our gut piles after we packed out the meat. We were not overly concerned, but decided we would hunt higher up the slopes just to avoid running into this fellow in the thick alders down at sea level. On that first climb, we fought our way up a nearly vertical ravine for a couple hundred feet to higher, but still sloping ground and were rewarded when a fat little forkhorn jumped up not far away. My companion promptly shot him and he slid right down the ravine we had just climbed. We edged over to a precipice to see where he had landed and saw (for the first time), the bear that had been following us around. He was carrying the forkhorn right back down the trail that had led us to the ravine we had climbed.

If you hunt in coastal Alaska, you soon learn that you may have to share your meat with the other predators in the area.

Bears can be frightening, yet if asked to sum up my feelings about bears in one anecdote it would not be a tale involving fear or danger. It would be the far simpler tale of a bear I once watched from the flying bridge of a Coast Guard Cutter in the early nineties, in a nameless cove down near the tip of the Alaska Peninsula. It was a warm evening in late summer and I found myself up on the flying bridge scanning the hills around us with a pair of enormous "big eye" binoculars mounted on a pedestal. I had not scanned very long when I saw a bear sitting on the edge of an overlook some distance away. The wonderful optics and clear air allowed me to see every detail of this animal even though he must have been nearly a half mile away. He was a big chocolate colored male who was already filled out with most of his fall fat, his coat glossy and thick.

I was struck by how oddly "human" the animal looked. He was seated on the edge of that knoll with his legs spread out downhill in the same attitude your obese uncle Wally might strike in his lounge chair, only lacking a TV remote and a can of beer to complete the picture. It wasn't only his appearance and posture, but his actions that lent him an odd air of humanity. He would lean forward and peer down the hill at unseen objects or at the boat - at me - with an expression of curiosity. Occasionally he would reach up and wave his paw in front of his face to bat away the gnats and mosquitoes. He would scratch his head or his "arm" pits then yawn and shift his position with the same lazy and ponderous movements that any recumbent and somewhat overweight gentleman might use in similar circumstances.

I was fascinated and amused by all of this body English, but the crowning moment came when he stuck the tip of his tongue out of the side of his mouth denoting great concentration on some supremely important task. I watched in anticipation as he shifted his buttocks and then reached into his itchy crotch to give it a nice scratch: Aaaahhhhh! He must have hit just the right spot because his tongue disappeared and his facial expression became one of contentment. He then reclined with his back against the hill, closed his eyes and went to sleep; his open mouth pointed at the sky, paws occasionally swinging up (perhaps unconsciously), to wave the bugs away from his face or scratch an itch. I left him to his nap and when I looked again sometime later, he was gone.

Until that time, I had never had occasion to watch a bear at ease like that. Bears normally relax in some brushy spot where they can observe the world around, yet remain invisible (or at least obscured) to the observer. Doubtless, this bear was simply harried by insects on this hot summer day and had chosen this comfortable perch above the beach to catch a little of the sea breeze. A human in the same place would have done the same thing in the same way and with the same mannerisms.

I do not want to be accused of anthropomorphism when I draw these comparisons. Bears are not humans, but evolution has a way of finding similar solutions to the same challenges. Bears sometimes act like humans because they fill the same ecological niche as our own ancestors. While our primate forebears adapted to the opportunistic lifestyle of the omnivore in Africa, the bear's progenitors had done the same in a colder part of the world. Like us, his brain grew to facilitate his exploratory lifestyle, his limbs changed into useful tools and weapons rather than a mere means of conveyance.

Bears and humans have a lot in common.

Chapter 5
People and Bears

People often react oddly to the presence of a bear. I have seen perfectly normal and well-adjusted people become completely unglued at an encounter with one of these animals. The reactions are often so extreme that I cannot help wondering if there is not something going on beneath the surface, some primitive dread or weird psychological phenomena.

It is not unusual for people in the suburbs of Anchorage to encounter the odd angry moose in the driveway, and perhaps even be chased 'round the rhododendrons for a while if the animal is feeling particularly feisty. Such events are retold with a lot of laughter and humorous embellishment, one of those events that are characterized as being merely colorful rather than terrifying or traumatic. Stories of this nature are picked up by the local paper and relegated to the Sunday edition with headlines like "Anchorage Grandmother Leaps SUV to Evade Moose." It is all very amusing and well worth a good chuckle when we come across the article (complete with color photo of the smiling Granny and the SUV in question), over a coffee on Sunday morning. Stories about recalcitrant wildlife are just part of everyday life for all of us. The scale may differ, but a moose in an Anchorage driveway or a raccoon in a New Jersey garage will elicit the same tolerance tempered with humor.

It is generally a very different story with bears. People often respond with a completely blind and unreasoning panic to an encounter with even a mild-tempered little black bear. A hungry grizzly slipping into a small town at night to raid the dumpsters can create hysteria out of all proportion to the actual danger the animal represents. Police and wildlife officials (usually under intense public pressure), are forced to respond by destroying the animal. This is a pattern I have seen repeatedly here in my own small town. It is not uncommon for bears to wander in and scavenge garbage or raid backyard fish smokehouses. This is particularly prevalent in the spring when bears exit the den, lean and hungry after a long winter. Local officials are equipped and trained to deal with such animals by using various noise making devices and/or pepper spray. This usually works quite well and it becomes an event of little consequence, a one-line item in the police blotter. However, all too often, an individual bear is particularly stubborn (or hungry) and hangs around until the inevitable public outcry takes shape.

Eventually, the bear (or its tracks) are seen near a playground or school bus stop and the animal's fate is sealed at the first cry of: "What about the children?" This is particularly sad when it is a sow with cubs - a very common scenario since a mother bear has a much greater incentive to risk human contact for food.

Of course, bears habituated to humans really can be dangerous and given enough time and contact, somebody may indeed be hurt or killed. Yet, that very real danger (as slight as it is) does not wholly explain the wildly unbalanced reactions that people have to the presence of these animals.

A friend of mine once told me a story about a personal bear encounter that occurred shortly after he had first arrived in Alaska. One warm summer day he and his wife were fishing in the Buskin River just outside of town when a young bear showed up across the stream from them. My friend was standing on the bank while his wife was out in the stream between him and the bear. The animal was calmly walking along the far side of the river, minding its own business and ignoring the numerous people in the area. My friend quietly drew his wife's attention to the animal, perhaps thinking she would be as fascinated as he would by this close encounter with the local wildlife. He was totally unprepared for her reaction – she immediately began shrieking, turned and literally knocked him down and ran over him over in a desperate flight to safety – the car in fact, parked several hundred yards away.

Surely, the creature was surprised and disturbed by the noisy female biped dashing into the woods across the stream, and perhaps puzzled by the male biped - cursing and floundering on the bank, with muddy footprints up his chest...

Another old friend of mine was a bear guide back in the 1940's and 50's. He told me a number of stories about various clients who had fallen completely apart when encountering their first brown bear.

It is one thing to know (in an intellectual way) how large a brown bear is, yet it is quite another to actually encounter one at close range for the first time and sense that unmistakable "presence." Seeing a grizzly in the distance is merely an opportunity to watch an object of interest, something to be enjoyed for the moment, but certainly not an experience that elicits any sort of visceral reaction from the casual observer. However, a brownie standing on the trail ten or twenty yards ahead of you falls into an entirely different realm of human experience. Suddenly, the superiority and control of the human species is snatched away by the cosmic pickpocket, leaving you at the mercy of another species of animal when you suddenly realize that in his world you are not at the top of the food chain. Will the bear walk away and allow you to live to an old age, or decide to end your life at that moment? Holding a heavy firearm in your grasp tends to even up the odds, but the experience of meeting a large bear at close range can still be shocking.

Any bear guide worth his fee will stalk up very close to a bear before allowing a client to take a shot. An ethical guide does not want wounded bears running around, especially since it will fall to him to track down and deliver the coup de grace should his client botch the shot. A wounded bear will invariably burrow into the deepest cover it can find, to lie watching its back-trail for any pursuit; plenty of incentive for a guide to give his client the cleanest shot possible. A good guide may spend hours bringing his hunter into close proximity to the bear by utilizing every fold of ground, every bit of brush, every minute change of wind to execute a stalk. It is often not until they find themselves at a range of ten or twenty yards that the client gets a good look at the animal they are hunting. This can result in some very odd reactions.

One story that sticks in my mind is of the hunter who rose (goggle-eyed) to face a bear at close range and without once pulling the trigger, simply worked the bolt on his rifle until all five shells in his magazine were ejected to land at his feet, unfired. He then turned to the guide and shouted, "My God, what does it take to kill one of those things?" The bear departed the area at high speed, and it was not until the guide picked up the unfired shells and showed them to the exasperated hunter, that he would believe he had not fired a shot.

Another hunter (in the same situation) rose, aimed his rifle and stood there for some time, before finally turning to the guide and simply saying "No." before walking away at a high rate of speed. When questioned later, he ruefully replied that he did not want to make an animal of that size angry, by shooting it.

Some hunters get the shakes so bad they simply miss their enormous target, even at the close ranges common to bear hunting. They often refuse to accept that fact when the guide explains that they simply missed and that the animal has departed unharmed (or perhaps merely deafened) by the fusillade of heavy rifle shots.

What is it about the bear that creates this sort of reaction? Obviously, in the case of brown bears we are talking about a very large predator indeed, a creature whose biological reality alone should create fear in a close encounter. Yet, there is something more here... I have talked about bears (and how we react to them) at some length, but let's take it a little further and give this some historical and cultural context.

Certain animals elicit this innate, instinctive, response from humans, and bears are certainly on that list. In the same way that stepping on a snake or hearing the song of wolves late at night will raise your hair and bring butterflies to your stomach; an encounter with a bear can create the very same visceral reaction. I have often wondered if this is something imprinted in the brainstem, some inner dread passed down from our distant forebears, an instinctive reaction rather than learned behavior.

Bears fill the same ecological niche as our early ancestors and more than any other animal were (and still are, in some places) in direct competition with man. They are opportunistic, omnivorous predators (as are we) who have always gravitated to the same sources of food that drew (and still draw) humans, across much of the northern hemisphere.

Bears and humans have a shared history from their earliest contact. When man was a hunter/gatherer, every food source from berries, bulbs and succulent plants to fish, game (or even carrion scavenged from other successful predators), put us in direct conflict with the bear. Of course, the omnivorous bear has the same adaptable seasonal habits as man. He too is a bit of a wanderer on the earth, a creature with no real fixed address or home territory. He is an omnivore drawn to the same places that drew early migratory human populations at the same times of year, and for the same reason: food. When early man gathered the first succulent greens of spring on south facing slopes, we shared that harvest with the bear. When we seasonally congregated on the rivers and tributaries of northern Europe, Asia and America to catch salmon or other spawning fish, so did the bear. In late summer when we moved to locales where wild fruits and berries could be gathered, there again was the bear. In Fall, when our forebears surrounded and killed wild cattle or horses on their migratory routes to winter ranges, there once more was the bear hunting those same ruminants, or drawn to the scene of our kills to contest ownership of the prize.

It must have occasioned a great deal of shock and disappointment when our ancestors moved north from Africa to meet their first bear. I can picture some Cro-Magnon chieftain moving his victorious band ever northward into the rich lands of Europe, strutting proudly, positively giddy with delight at the new-found plethora of water and food, only to be appalled when a ton of cave bear suddenly loped out of the berry

bushes to carry away one of his lumpy lieuten-
ants. The arid steppes of northern Africa must
not have seemed so bad in hindsight. Perhaps
our beetle-browed Rommel then regretted not
staying home and going into the flint-knapping
trade as his uncle Ted had advised him so long
ago.

Indeed, in the depths of Africa man had
evolved for millions of years into a kind of su-
per-animal. A creature that hunted animals
like any predator, but could also graze on green
vegetation or seeds like the ruminants, climb
trees to gather fruit, net fish from the rivers and
streams. He was animal with no specialization;
a magnificent creature that could adapt to any
situation or survive any of the natural catastro-
phes that periodically decimated other wildlife
populations. Furthermore, his brain was developed enough to allow him to break free from
the chains of instinct that kept other creatures
rooted in home territories or on seasonal mi-
grations that might be a trail to disaster in a giv-
en year. Man was free of all that; free to seek out
and explore new lands when forced by drought
or over-population. There is nothing else quite

like that in Africa – no other animal to challenge man's preeminence in all things. A lion or leopard has a territory and if they became bothersome, early man could simply relocate to another area to leave his enemy outside the animals range. On the other hand, the creature could simply be surrounded and killed with spears, as the Masai do even today. Even the largest cat is small enough to be dealt with by a group of spear wielding hunters.

That changed when man entered Europe. The northern lands already had an animal with many of the same attributes as man. There were two varieties of bear in Europe at that time, the same European Brown Bear (Ursus Arctos) that we know today, along with his larger cousin the Cave Bear (Ursa Spelaeus) an enormous animal approximating the size of the modern Alaskan Brown Bear; formidable creatures both, and far larger than any predator that man had faced in warmer climes. Wherever man went in the new lands, he did so in dread of meeting a bear, his constant competitor and his equal in the battle for survival. Man may have had a slight strategic advantage with his tools and his tendency to hunt in groups, but it is hard to imagine even a sizable group of humans armed with flint-tipped spears, coming off well after an encounter with a large bear.

The seasonal homes of our nomadic early ancestors were certainly not safe from bear incursions. The dwelling places of our ragged forebears must have been a magnet for bears, with a variety of pungent food odors wafting away on the wind as an olfactory invitation. Such a place would have been a veritable cornucopia for any enterprising predator, but especially for a bear, whose great size gave him some immunity from the primitive weapons of early man. Wolves might be kept at bay with a club or a flint spear, but not a ton of cave bear.

Doubtless, early man was a common item on the menu of the bear. Perhaps he was a troublesome entrée who could only be had at the cost of some painful jabs with flint-tipped spears, but an entrée nonetheless whenever an easier meal could not be found. For thousands of generations Cro-Magnon and later Homo Sapiens, huddled around fires and talked of bears, plotted defense against bears, told of narrow escapes from bears and mourned the loss of loved ones to bears.

In light of this, we should not be surprised when examining European mythology to discover that the actual wild creatures that we fear today are the same ones encountered in somewhat fanciful fashion throughout the folklore passed down through the ages. Isn't a dragon (which was portrayed as a legless snake-like creature until a few generations ago) just a wildly enhanced version of the common European adders and vipers that have killed unwary children throughout European history? We certainly react to snakes with an instinctive dread. If you doubt that, ask any Boy Scout what happens when you rustle a twig in the grass next to somebody and yell "Snake!" What of the werewolf? Aren't the various wolf and dog-like monsters just a supernatural version of the same wild canines that still prompt us to throw extra wood on the campfire when their song is heard late at night? There is always the bear, the central figure in so much of our folklore and campfire tales.

When primitive man killed a bear (which he undoubtedly did upon occasion) and took the rich pelt as a prize, he would have been faced with the same unsettling sight that greets modern hunters. The denuded bear carcass resembles nothing so much as a human form; a man wrapped in the skin of a beast. With the exception of the skull, a bear carcass looks quite human in nearly every detail. Every northern culture shares the myth of the big hairy man-like "thing" of the forest and mountains - the slavering monster that lived out there beyond our ken, just past the hill or stream that marked the known boundary of the village world. He has different names in different cultures; he was variously Ogre, Troll, Grendel or a hundred other names in European tongues. In central Asia he was Alma, in Tibet; Yeti. In the new world, he is the Sasquatch or Ohlock.

No matter the name, he is the same creature - the Boogeyman that steals your cache of winter-stored grain, drags your last sheep away into the forest, your child from its cradle or your wife from the berry patch. An envious and malignant creature who begrudges you your warm shelter and the food you have carefully stored away – the food that spells the difference between life and death in the coming winter. This creature is shaped like an enormous hairy human being. He is strong and cunning and can walk on two legs, but he just doesn't smell right. He does not have the good smell of wood smoke overlaid with the congested funk of crowded and unwashed humanity. No, he carries an entirely different smell, the scent of wilderness.

He is definitely not one of us.

He was always there in the darkness just beyond the firelight where our ancestors gathered to tell tales. He was there when Cro-Magnon man first found his way north from Africa and during the ice age when the first modern men huddled around fire at the mouth of French caves. He was still there when the ice retreated and modern man learned to sow wild grains and store this food-treasure for the winter. Eventually, those tales were written down and fixed into our consciousness as the folklore we all share even today; the bedtime stories that underlie our childhood nightmares. It was of course, the people in the walled towns of

18th century Europe who wrote the tales down rather than the people in distant villages who still huddled at the edge of wilderness. I suspect that if the Brothers Grimm had gathered their tales from the foothills of the Alps (instead of tame and tidy Hesse), our mythical monsters would be more clearly recognized as the bear that shaped the original tales.

The monster that comes down to us in such similar fashion from so many parts of Europe, Asia and North America is indeed the bear - that same omnivorous, opportunistic, (sometimes bipedal) predator that gave Cro-Magnon man the vapors. He was still out there in the European hinterland, still roaming the edge of distant fields at night, still drawn by the ripe smells of our refuse piles and food storehouses, still eyeing our cattle and sheep as an easy meal. Maybe the barking dogs or the flimsy fence would keep him away, or maybe he would bust right in and take what he wanted, and kill anyone foolish enough to try and stop him. Sometimes a hunter would fail to return home. Occasionally, a woman or child would disappear, leaving only an empty berry basket and a set of impossibly large and man-like tracks leading into the forest to provide the only clue to their terrible fate.

The most terrifying folklore is drawn from the dread that resides deep in our guts - that eternal fear that springs from utter helplessness in the face of malignant powers beyond our strength and understanding. Evil and powerful kings, witches who cast magical spells, and always the various supernatural beasts; the malevolent, cunning and powerful creatures who live in the dark forest beyond the pasture and cultivated land we call our own; out there in the dark forests where man cannot claim to be at the top of the food chain. All of these tales began with some sort of reality, but as they were passed down the details become hazy, the origin obscure. By the time the Brothers Grimm began recording these stories, bears were rare creatures in much of Europe. The eternal nemesis who stalked the edge of our villages (and our nightmares) had morphed into something magical, but still recognizable as the wild creature we know today. We have merely to strip away the storyteller's veneer of supernatural attributes to reveal the actual living creature beneath the surface.

The tales are not always dark. One can often find hope and instruction when they reveal the weaknesses of the monster. Indeed, as fearsome as he is, the creature is not all-powerful. If a warrior is brave or smart enough he can kill the beast and save the beautiful young maiden or the child. The monster may be cunning, but he can be tricked into doing something foolish if you are quick-witted enough. He will throw himself onto your spear if you goad him, as will the bear. You can climb a tree or feign death to escape the monster, just as you might do with a bear - the European brown bear (like the American grizzly), cannot climb trees. The Scandinavian Troll falls into a heavy stupor in daylight in the same fashion as the bear in winter. Indeed, that is how the Scandinavians hunted bear until very recent times, finding the winter den and awakening the bear to exit into the face of iron-tipped spears.

American history is filled with bear tales from the very first landings along the east coast. Those eastern bears would have been the black bear, but it is obvious those early settlers took them quite seriously. One wonders if the black bears of that day were more aggressive than the bears found in the east today. It certainly appears that black bears in the west and Alaska are somewhat more aggressive than eastern bears. Perhaps those black bears with aggressive genes were simply killed off over the years in areas where they have lots of human contact. Alternatively, have these bears simply adapted to increased human presence by using avoidance rather than aggression?

The first well-recorded contact with the American grizzly is found in the journals of Lewis and Clark. Oddly, they referred to them as "white bears" though they were undoubtedly of a light brown color. There is some evidence that a distinct sub-species of large, light brown grizzlies lived around the breaks of the Missouri subsisting on fish, and these were undoubtedly what they encountered.

"We now found ourselves in the land of the big bears along the upper Missouri River."

"... The hunters killed 3 white bear one large, the fore feet of which measured 9 Inchs across, the hind feet 11 Inchs ¾ long & 7 Inch's wide a bear nearly Catching Joseph Fields Chased him into the water, bear about the Camp every night & Seen on an Isld. in the day."

...'One day one of their hunters came running into camp out of breath and with much fear in his face. "I shot the critter, but he just kept on coming at me. I just barely escaped with my life."

They formed a party and went after the creature to dispatch it. They found it in a thicket and managed to kill it, but were amazed at its endurance after the first man's shot; it had managed to travel a considerable distance...

They tried different methods of hunting the big bears. They would have four men fire while holding two riflemen in reserve for more firing if needed - and it was nearly always needed. Even though the bears were shot through the lungs and sometimes even in the heart, they would keep coming. The only sure shot they found was to the brain but that was not easy, because the skull was covered with thick muscle.

"Once a wounded giant bear chased two of our hunters off a twenty foot bluff into the river...and itself plunged into the water and swam after them.

It was fortunately killed with a lucky head shot by a rifleman on shore. The explorers felt that nothing should stop their mission, and they had to try and exert domination over every aspect of nature from weather to these incredible new bears they had discovered inhabiting the west. This struggle with the bears became as formidable as the river or the hostile natives or the incredible distances they had to cover to complete their mission.

The party needed the big bears for oil, fat, food and hides. They would cook with the oil and use the fat for caulking their boats. They also saved the fat for use later on the axles and crude wheels to transport boats on trams during portage. The hides made warm blankets and robes.

These brown bears of the west soon came to be known as grizzlies (after the more common color found in the mountains), their power and strength become the stuff of legend, and myth as succeeding generations opened up the continent. The rifles used in the east in those early days (the "Kentucky" or "Pennsylvania" rifle) were of small caliber and fired balls of perhaps .36 caliber and weighing 90 grains or so. Even the larger rifles commonly fired .45 caliber balls of 145 grains in weight, quite insufficient for dealing with a grizzly. After about 1830, the Hawken rifle became the rifle of choice for westerners. This rifle was made in St. Louis specifically for the western trade and featured bore sizes from .54 to as large as .68 caliber with an exponential increase in the weight of the balls fired. Still, these were muzzleloaders and you were only going to get one shot. It is easy to understand why the grizzly was feared and respected by early settlers and hunters.

There is an entire mythology built around the grizzly in the western US and everyone from Mark Twain to Teddy Roosevelt contributed to the pool of sometimes-true stories and legends.

One of the most interesting man-bear tales I know of comes from Europe; the story of Wojtek (pronounced Voytek) the Polish soldier bear. In 1939, Poland was invaded from two sides by the Germans and the Soviet Union. The Polish army fought bravely but was soon overwhelmed by its larger neighbors. Soldiers captured by the Soviet Union suffered a particularly awful fate as the entire officer corps of 22,000 men were taken away and systematically executed by the NKVD in the forest at Katyn, near Smolensk. The enlisted men's fate was not much better - they were exported to grim Soviet Gulags in Siberia to be used as forced labor in mines and logging camps under conditions that can hardly be imagined.

In 1942, this situation changed. The German-Soviet alliance was broken and now these countries were at war, with German armies cutting deep into Soviet territory. Stalin decided to release any Polish prisoners who would volunteer to fight the Germans. Of course, few of them wanted to fight with the Soviets, so a deal was arranged with the British who would incorporate them into their army. Over 100,000 of these battered Polish soldiers began making their way south from various points in the USSR to meet the British in what is now Iraq. Somewhere in the mountains of Persia (now Iran), some of these men came across a young boy with a starving brown bear cub whose mother had been shot. Perhaps reminded of their own recent situation, these soldiers took pity on the captive animal and purchased it with tins of preserved meat they were carrying for their own rations. He must have been about two years old then, as pictures taken in 1944 show him as a young adult bear.

The bear was dubbed Wojtek, a Polish name rooted in old Slavonic that means something like "Happy Warrior." The young bear was taken along and proved a good comrade who enjoyed the same rations as the soldiers, with a particular fondness for condensed milk as an after dinner treat.

In Iraq, the British organized their new soldiers into various units and Wojtek ended up in the 22nd Transport Company, Artillery Division of the Polish 2nd Corps. Two young men named Henryk and Dymitr from the 4th Platoon took charge of him and saw that he was fed and bathed - he was allowed into the bathhouse at certain hours and much enjoyed being soaped and scrubbed. He eventually learned how to turn on the faucets by himself and would visit the bathhouse on his own during the heat of the day for a cool shower. The 4th Platoon also had a pet monkey named Kasha and a dog named Kirkuk. The three animals became fast friends. At some point during this training and organizational period, the monkey died in some accident and Wojtek was inconsolable for a time. Then Kirkuk was stung by a scorpion and also died. It may have been at this time that Henryk and Dymitr introduced the sad Wojtek to beer. Beer was an instant hit with the bear and he could drink it just like a person straight from the bottle, finishing by carefully eyeing the contents when it was empty to make sure he had gotten every drop. He had such a fondness for beer that the Company had to lock it up to keep him from stealing it, later rationing him to just two bottles a day "for his health." Wojtek himself was badly stung on the nose by a scorpion and the subsequent swelling nearly cut off his breathing. Intervention by a British army surgeon and nursing care by his friend Henryk soon had him back to normal.

Wojtek also developed a fondness for cigarettes, eating them at first and then learning to smoke. Soldiers would give him a lit cigarette and he would sit with them in the evenings and enjoy his tobacco and friends. That sounds quite unbelievable, but many years later Wojtek ended up in the Edinburg zoo and the former Polish soldiers that had settled in Scotland would visit him and toss him lit cigarettes to smoke and enjoy; a scene witnessed by thousands of people over the years. Wojtek's most preferred recreation seemed to center on wrestling and many of the men would accommodate him in this pastime, stopping by at all hours of the day and evening to have a wrestle with Wojtek. Nobody could beat him of course, but after a friendly tussle and a few hugs and kisses, they would part as friends until the next challenge. It was all skittles and beer for the soldier bear in those early days.

The new Polish Corps was soon moved to Palestine and one night when Wojtek went to play in the bathhouse he chased a hiding Arab out who was soon subdued by a couple of soldiers. Wojtek was credited with capturing a spy, though in all likelihood the poor fellow was just a common thief. Nevertheless, the incident made him locally famous around the Polish Corps and the larger British 8th Army.

The British army was adamantly opposed to pets (at least on paper) of all kinds and issued an order to the Polish Corps on the subject as training ended. All the pets would have to be left behind when the unit pulled out to join the action in late 1943. The issue was resolved by enlisting Wojtek as a soldier with the rank of Private, his own pay book and serial number. There was apparently a dispute of some kind when they reached Egypt and began embarkation on a ship, but once Wojtek's papers were presented the British bureaucrat soon relented and Wojtek was off to war with the British 8th Army. He was now close to four years of age and stood about six feet tall on his hind legs. Pictures taken later show he eventually reached a height of just over seven feet if the scale of his human companions is a good gauge, about average for a European brown bear. At that size, in his prime, he probably weighed near 600 pounds.

The Polish 2nd Corps ended up on the Italian front supporting the allied push up the peninsula and this is where Wojtek gained his greatest fame. He seemed to have absolutely no fear of shellfire and happily rode in the truck with the rumblings of war all around him. Thousands of British and American soldiers were stunned and amused to see a truck of the 22nd Transport Company go by with a bear riding in the passenger seat or perched on crates in the back of a truck. He was generally described with his head sticking from the window, interested in all the various sights and smells passing him by. The Company was now moving day by day and the Poles began to worry that he might get frightened or injured in one of the many artillery bombardments and run off and be lost. His friend Henryk had been designated as an artillery observer and was frequently not there to keep Wojtek in line. Somebody fashioned a comfortable leather collar for him and they began chaining him up to one the supply trucks when Henryk was not around to watch after him. One of the heavy items they were transporting were large boxes of artillery shells, which took several men to lift onto a truck and Wojtek, found these exertions by the men very interesting. Observing that interest, his pals soon had Wojtek lifting these onto the trucks as part of the loading team. He enjoyed it and proved extremely useful, so much so that the company adopted a Logo of a bear carrying an artillery shell and this was soon painted on all the vehicles and worn as a badge on their uniforms.

His most famous exploits were along the Gustav Line and Monte Cassino in 1944. This was a nearly impregnable defensive position the Germans had established along the high ground south of Rome to bottle the allies up in southern Italy. The allies threw themselves at this line for months in a series of costly battles. Allied artillery fire was continuous and millions of shells were transported to the front. Wojtek worked all through this period loading trucks with his Polish friends, and drinking beer and smoking cigarettes with them whenever they got a break.

When the war ended, the Polish Corps were transferred to the village of Hutton in Berwickshire, Scotland, and of course, Wojtek went along with them and became a favorite at the many local pubs favored by the soldiers. I suppose even a canny Scotsman might spring for a pint when a 500 pound bear sits next to him. In 1947, the unit was finally disbanded and many of the Poles elected to stay in the UK instead of going home to a Poland under Soviet control. His comrades sadly decided that the best course of action was to send Wojtek to the Edinburg zoo, where he lived until his death in 1963. It is said he became rather quiet and withdrawn there unless he heard Polish spoken, which was a frequent occurrence since many of his old comrades would visit him whenever they could. When he heard Polish, he would become animated and interact with whomever was speaking. Wojtek had a way of shaking his head when he wanted a cigarette, and he would make this signal whenever he heard the Polish language. Most of his old friends would toss him lit cigarettes and occasionally somebody would climb over the rails and wrestle with him for a while until some official chased them out.

During those years, he became locally famous and would appear on TV shows. Somebody wrote a children's book about him. He died in 1963 and is now largely forgotten by all but the few surviving old Polish soldiers who served with him.

Here on Kodiak, the Koniag/Alutiiq people are close enough to their hunter-gatherer roots that we can still hear the original tales, as they must have been told long ago. These tales are very similar to the European bear and monster tales, only differing in that more often the protagonist is clearly a bear. The bear of the Koniag is variously an evil nemesis or conversely, an almost sympathetic figure, lonely and somewhat envious of the comforts of the roomy barabara where our Koniag hero resides in warmth and comfort. He may disguise himself and live among us until his true nature is revealed by the Shaman. He may steal a woman away to his lonely cave to be his mate and to give him the comforts he lacks. Much like the European monster/bear, he can be out-witted by a clever hunter.

I heard many old tales from my friend Hank, a wonderful old guy who had grown up in Ouzinkie village on neighboring Spruce Island, in the early part of the last century. He had been a bear hunting guide back in the early days and in fact, is the source for much of the hunting guide material presented earlier in the book. Sadly, Hank passed on to new realms a few years ago, leaving me to wistfully recall the many winter afternoons spent in his warm kitchen drinking his strong black tea. Most of those hours were spent listening to this amazing man tell me things that can only be learned with eighty years of hard work in an unforgiving land. He told me of poverty and hardship that are difficult to comprehend today. He lived through natural disasters; the tidal waves, earthquakes and volcanic eruptions that have devastated this remote coast. He lived through the Thousand Mile War - the Japanese invasion of Alaska where Aleutian villagers were dragged away to the Japanese mainland to die in slave labor camps, while others were torn away (for their own good...) by our own government to die of tuberculosis and neglect in camps far from their island homes. Hank had witnessed firsthand the amazing history of Alaska in the 20th century.

When he was about 12 years of age his mother would send him out to shoot a bear in the spring. Spring bear meat is lean and mild tasting and natives normally only hunted them at that time of year. The family rifle was an old Winchester .25/35 that still he owned when I came to know him. Anyway, his Mom would send him out armed with a half dozen rounds of those tiny cartridges to kill a bear to feed them until the salmon came in.

I was intrigued by this and asked him how somebody could kill a Kodiak bear with such an inadequate cartridge. His answer was straightforward, in that he'd just get as close as possible, reveal himself and then shoot the bear through the mouth for a brain or upper spine shot (depending on the angle of the bruins head). I asked him what would happen if he missed and he just looked at me with a shocked expression and said, "Oh, you wouldn't want to miss!"

More importantly (for our purposes here), Hank had an almost encyclopedic knowledge of the folklore and mythology of his Alutiiq people, rich tales every bit as complex and fascinating as the more familiar stories of my own European tradition. Sometimes that folklore cannot quite be separated from actual events. I heard some very odd stories indeed; things that can only be accepted on the veracity of the person telling the tale since they cannot be proven in an objective fashion – tales of bizarre sea creatures, supernatural occurrences and of something else that sounded quite familiar to me...

He told me of a creature that had both entertained and frightened him as a child. The *Ohlock; an enormous, hairy, smelly, man-like creature that only differed from the bear in that he was entirely bipedal and had the face of a man (or ape). Just like the bear, he would steal your winter food cache or kill an unwary hunter or berry-picker - or steal a child from its bed. Just as in Europe, Alutiiq children were put to sleep with frightening tales of this creature. Sometimes Ohlock is described as the offspring of a bear and a human woman.

This is usually pronounced; "Oorluck" and there are a number of spelling variations. It is

quite possible that the name "Ohlock" may be a case of cultural cross-contamination from the Russians who ruled Kodiak for many years. Ohlock (Oorluck) sounds suspiciously like Orlok (the title for a Mongol commander), and fearful tales of the Mongol horde are common in Russian folklore. Therefore, it would not surprise me if the term Orlok/Oorluck was not once used to designate some awful creature the Russians used to terrify children at bedtime - a name left behind in the hinterlands of Russian Alaska.

No matter the origin of the name, Hank assured me that the stories of the creature itself dated back to a period long before the Russians came. There is a striking similarity between Hank's childhood Ohlock and my own bedtime nemesis, the Boogeyman. The Boogeyman was the creature that my Appalachian grandmother used to frighten me with on an almost nightly basis - it is a wonder any kid raised prior to Dr. Seuss was able to function without chemical sedation and electro-shock therapy. These tales reveal how deeply ingrained into our psyche this man/bear/thing really is, and in what similar fashion various cultures dealt with him. The Boogeyman of my grandmother comes from the Irish/British tradition. Hank's Ohlock comes variously from the Russian/Aleut/Koniag/Alutiiq tradition, yet this is clearly the very same beast. The same creature of folklore found in every culture around the northern hemisphere – in every society where the bear's historic range overlapped with man. The creature leaps across continents and cultures, time and space, to shape the folklore (and the nightmares) of the northern world. The same facade of myth and magic are woven to create the same monster - the thing that walks like a man but thinks like a bear.

It is worth noting that there are reports of actual sightings of Ohlock in (relatively) recent history, by some quite sober and respectable people. One example occurred in the 1970's when the crew of a fishing boat put in to the lee of Tonki Cape (on nearby Afognak Island) to escape a bad winter storm. Looking ashore, they witnessed a large bipedal creature striding across a snowfield above the beach and concluded that they were seeing a man who might need help, considering the very remote locale. They put ashore to investigate and offer assistance but only found some enormous foot-prints in the snow; prints much larger than any man could make. They concluded they had seen an Ohlock, based on the fact that it was winter when bears are supposed to be hibernating - and of course because the creature had walked on its hind legs.

These were hard-working fishermen; sober realists who are not easily led into flights of fancy. Part of me would like to believe that there really is some enormous creature out there; a creature canny enough to hide from the prying eyes of man and remain unknown to science. Yet, I know that is not true... these men had seen a bear.

We know that coastal Alaskan bears do exit the den in winter, sometimes for long periods. We also know that bears can walk on their hind legs, though it is difficult to fathom why this one was doing so. Perhaps in this wild storm the bears den had been swept away in an avalanche (a common enough event), and it is possible that the bear's front legs had been injured in the course of this same catastrophe. We can only speculate.

I am not interested in pursuing mythical creatures – such tales (for me) are more interesting for what they reveal about the thin line between mythology and reality in the human mind. The door in our brain that separates myth from reality is not entirely closed and we all (like these fishermen) can witness a real event and interpret it in favor of the magical, rather than the merely unusual.

In light of all this, it is not surprising that yelling "bear" in a dark tent late at night will create universal bedlam and related bedwetting. It is not surprising that Alaskan tourist's (and even locals who should know better) often react in an almost hysterical fashion to the presence of a bear.

I am reminded of coming across some French tourists fishing in the remote Karluk River at the south end of Kodiak one summer. These people had flown two heavily armed local "bear guards" out there with them to stand at the ready while they fished - good work if you can get it.

While a firearm is not out of place on a wilderness fishing trip, this looked more like an Israeli incursion into the West Bank than a recreational activity. The "guards" were playing the part by maintaining a serious demeanor behind mirrored sunglasses (to demonstrate their cool professionalism...) as they stood on the hillside above, or escorted the Frenchmen up and down the riverbank - guns always at the ready.

I had opportunity to chat with one of the anglers and learned that he was an executive in a large French liquor concern. He had fished Kodiak several times in the past and on one of those trips had encountered a bear at close range. He was frank in admitting that the event had been terrifying and traumatic for him even though nobody had been injured or even threatened by the animal. The size of the bear alone had been enough to completely shatter him. Hence, there were the expensive armed guards to accompany him and his friends on their annual fishing sojourn; a cost they bore happily enough simply for peace of mind.

It is difficult to *completely* reject this sort of reaction as unreasoning paranoia, because people are indeed occasionally attacked and killed by bears - and quite honestly, the sheer *scale* of a Kodiak bear will equal or surpass any fears drawn from our collective subconscious. Indeed, all of that inner dread is based on the European brown bear, an animal only half the size of an Alaskan Brown Bear and far less predatory in nature.

Perhaps this Frenchman's tales to his grandchild will be passed along and introduce a new element to the family bedtime stories; an industrial sized Boogeyman that smells of fish and a brave warrior with mirrored sunglasses...

Chapter 6
The Hunt

The hunt had taken shape like many others, originating in a bull session with friends and co-workers months before. My friend and hunting partncr of long duration was a genial bear of a man named Ira Kessler. Ira and I had hunted deer and caribou together many times, as well as fished, hiked and camped all across Alaska. We had spent so much time together that we had a mental inventory of each other's gear and knew from long habit who would bring what, and how we'd set about each new enterprise. Ira was the gadget guy, always supplied with the latest featherweight stove, high-tech radio or global positioning system. I was the traditionalist, bringing sturdy old enameled cookware and military frame packs. At some point that summer, we had decided to do a late season deer hunt out on the Kodiak refuge that began some miles southwest of our home. Like most of Alaska, there are no roads and access is by floatplane or boat.

In pricing a charter plane, we had determined that a team of four would be the most economical way to balance cost versus allowable weight. We soon found two additional friends to fill out our hunting party. Chuck Garwood and Brian Painter were younger co-workers of ours from the Coast Guard clinic. All four of us were experienced in emergency medicine, a fortuitous coincidence.

Floatplanes are chartered by the hour with the cost dependent on the size of the plane and the distance to be covered. The ubiquitous De-Havilland Beaver is the largest floatplane suitable for our purposes, capable of hauling a party

of four along with their equipment and harvested meat in one trip. These marvelous old air-
planes have not been manufactured for some
40 years, yet there are still thousands of them
in use across Alaska and western Canada. No
other aircraft can carry the payload, or has the
rugged dependability and versatility of these
old warhorses. Even considering the aging nature of these old birds, no other small plane can
touch their safety record in bush flying. When
the last of these old planes is gone, the nature
of Alaska itself will change.

The cost of the flight is calculated both ways,
meaning that a thirty-minute flight to a destination will cost you the additional time the pilot must fly back to his base – one hour. Since
an hour is the shortest period you can hire a
plane, we simply drew a circle on map to see
what would be inside the thirty-minute range
of a Beaver. That circle encompassed Uganik
Island, a large piece of land enclosed between
Viekoda and Uganik bays and separated from
the mainland at its southern end by a deep narrow fiord known as Terror bay. On our topographical maps, the southern tip of the island

appeared to have several beaches that would offer easy floatplane access as well as level ground above the beach to set up a camp. Inland a short distance, long spurs came down from the heights, appearing to offer (relatively) easy access to the high country where the best deer hunting would be found.

Just across the narrow channel from our chosen site was the mouth of a long fiord stretching deeper into the interior. To this day, I still do not know what dark event gave Terror Bay its unusual name.

We chose to do the hunt in late November for several reasons. Blacktails are largely mountain deer and the later in the season one hunts them, the greater the odds that high-country snow will have driven them to lower elevations, thus increasing the odds of success. You can also minimize bear contact by hunting late in the season when many of the animals have retreated to their dens.

As is often the case in Kodiak, the weather that year was uncooperative. A series of warm low-pressure fronts kept the island wet and (relatively) warm, too mild for snow even at higher elevations. By the eve of our hunt, very little snow had yet fallen in the high country and we simply resigned ourselves to a daily climb up into the alpine.

Saturday, November 21st found us unloading our gear under welcome (if unexpected), sunny skies and colder temperatures. The terrain above the beach was flat and sheltered by a grove of enormous spruce trees, perfect since our sunny weather was accompanied by chill NW wind. We set up camp in the lee of the trees, grateful for the windbreak. Inland, we could see a landscape of small hills densely covered with alders gradually rising to a steep escarpment topped with rocky pinnacles.

Days are short at that time of year and by the time we had set up camp and gathered a small supply of wood, there was no time to hunt. Night found us huddled around a fire in the spruce grove, sheltered (somewhat) from the cold wind. A bottle of Old Bushmills appeared and made the rounds, fueling our tongues and warding off snakebite. Of course, there are no snakes in Alaska, but one can never be too careful - and mild Irish whisky never tastes better than in an enameled cup under a crisp arctic sky.

We told some stories about past hunts. Ira and myself had a large fund of Alaska hunting stories to relate; some wildly funny, some hairy-chested, some of them even true. Brian had been in Alaska for a number of years as well, and had considerable backcountry experience. Chuck, in contrast, was a relative novice, having only hunted in the lower 48. His experiences were limited to much tamer country, but he was eager to get out into the real bush and broaden his horizons.

Ira told the story of a hunt we had made together a few years before. We (along with a third companion), had flown into the Mulchatna region of southwest Alaska to hunt caribou. Any time you find yourself deposited deep in the Alaskan wilderness you can count on running into a myriad of unexpected, bizarre, miserable, life-threatening and sometimes comical situations that all tie together into what we in Alaska like to call "hunting trips." That particular trip had more than the usual share of chaos and suffering. A few years had passed and those memories were now merely amusing, rather than painful. Much of the terrain in the Mulchatna country is a morass of muskeg flats that humans are not well equipped to walk on. The ground water melts in summer yet is prevented from draining by the permafrost only a few feet down to create an awful terrain known as muskeg. Muskeg is a thick soup covered by lichen growth that can be traversed only with some difficulty – it is like walking across a waterbed, something that is possible only as long as you don't punch through. However, when you strap 70 pounds of caribou meat to your back it becomes an almost insurmountable task, each step tending to break through the thin crust into the morass underneath and then requiring considerable force to "break suction" and extract your foot for the next step. We learned this fact after we had shot several caribou some miles from camp. We had then spent three days of backbreaking misery to haul all of that meat back to the lake where we camped.

On the first day of that epic of misery, we had neglected to bring enough water. Water is not usually much of a consideration in "our" part of Alaska where clear springs seem to gush from every hillside. However, that was not the case in the Mulchatna where the water was the color of weak coffee and crawling with tiny animals you could see with the naked eye. We were soon suffering from the effects of dehydration. To make matters worse, this was a late August hunt and the weather (even for that time of year) was unusually hot. Temperatures were in the eighties and we learned that it is an odd sensation to be standing in waist-deep water only a few degrees above freezing while your upper body is being roasted under a hot sun...

To top off that little adventure, our pilot did not appear on the scheduled date to pick us up. This is fairly typical of such hunts so we weren't overly concerned, knowing that even though the weather was fine in our locale, things may be very different in the mountain passes between us and Anchorage. Bush flying is predicated on the knowledge that a pilot is not going to risk his (or your) life flying in marginal weather. Your trip home is dependent on weather rather than on any schedule made in advance. We waited four days past our "scheduled" pick up and on the last day were reduced to barbecu-ing caribou on a stick over the fire – not bad actually, though the meat was quickly passing the point of "well-aged!" He did appear at last, to inform us that he had been diverted from a morning pick up (of us) to aid in a search for a lost party and was now low on fuel. We did not give that much thought until we groaned off the lake loaded with perhaps 1500 pounds of caribou meat, four large people and several hundred pounds of gear.

We began the long climb up the slopes of the Alaska Range only to run into a stiff headwind in the pass that slowed us down to a crawl and ate further into our low reserves of fuel! The pi-lot was beginning to act nervous and informed us that he was afraid the wind would only get worse at the top of the pass and if so, he would be forced to "dead stick" down the far side and hopefully, reach a lake near the bottom... At the moment he told us this, we were droning steadily up a narrow chasm with cliffs only a few hundred feet off each wing. There was no turning around.

To our relief, the winds decreased somewhat as we got higher and stopped abruptly at the top. The pilot cut the engine back and eased us down the far side of the range some eight or ten miles to sea level, where he fired up his engine and shot across Cook Inlet to Anchorage, setting down (finally) at his base lake, with fuel tanks nearly empty.

That trip may have been stranger and more strenuous than the average hunting trip, but Alaska is always an adventure. When you leave the road system, you are truly on your own; anything can happen and something usually does. It is all part of the Alaska backcountry package, with misery, er, "adventure" tossed in at no extra cost.

One of the things that make Kodiak hunting such a treat is the presence of an incredible number of grizzlies. There is nowhere else on the planet where these creatures live in such population densities, nor grow to the stupendous size found here. After a few encounters with these enormous (and often testy) animals you begin to lose your fear and look forward to their presence as a sort of icing on the cake; the element of danger that colors the entire experience in some elemental way – the "adventure" part of the hunting trip.

Much of our conversation that first night revolved around bears and bear experiences. We sat up late into the night huddled around the fire chatting about bears and past hunting trips.

I must confess here that on the following morning I awoke with a dull headache, at least partially due to the consumption of too much snakebite medicine on the previous night. Everyone else was eager to go, having (apparently) felt relatively snake-proof well before I had. Since someone would need to stay in camp and take care of some general housekeeping duties, I volunteered for the task. It was apparent we would need a great amount of firewood, and the foodstuffs needed to be moved away from camp and suspended in trees so as not to tempt bears – things we had not had time to do in the gathering darkness of the day before. At any rate, I elected to stay and take care of these chores - which I did after first fortifying myself with several cups of coffee and a half dozen aspirin.

By late morning, I had camp well set up and since my friends had still not returned and feeling bored, set out for some hunting and exploring on my own. It quickly became apparent that the low country around camp was very difficult terrain to hunt. A series of almost impenetrable alder thickets blanketed the low hills, broken by occasional stands of old spruce trees. The best way to traverse the country was by zigzagging from spruce grove to spruce grove following faint game tracks that forced me to crouch and even crawl through the thickets. Once among the giant spruces, the ground became clear and I could cover some distance until faced with another alder jungle. In several hours, I probably traveled less than a mile (as the crow flies) from camp, but covered many more miles in a circuitous route higher and higher in an attempt to get above the alder belt. I saw no deer and very little sign of them in all that country.

When I got back to camp, I was cheered by the news that the others had found a route to the base of a long spur offering access to the high country. They too had followed a circuitous route to that point and so hadn't had time to explore further before dark, but had sensibly laid out a route back to camp that would give us relatively quick access in the morning. We were further buoyed by the fact that the bitterly cold wind chose that evening to die down. We were treated to a still night under stars as crisp and clear as a desert sky. Having (now) a generous supply of wood, we were able to sustain a larger fire. Perhaps because of the snake-discouraging presence of that large fire, the Old Bushmills stayed packed away.

I recall that a pair of whales showed up that night and began a noisy display just offshore. We could not see them, but their loud exhalations punctuated the conversation, startling us repeatedly in the otherwise silent night.

We were up well before dawn gulping hot coffee and oatmeal prepared on a butane stove. On this day, Ira elected to stay in camp to cut a store of wood and take care of the various housekeeping chores. The rest of us (Brian, Chuck and I) stuffed some food and water in our frame packs and set off as soon as the first light of day allowed us to see the trail, my friends leading the way to the spur they'd found the day before.

We zigzagged west through the dense growth until eventually we reached the base of a long finger coming down off the mountain.

As is usually the case, there was a heavily used game trail leading up the spine of that finger. Wildlife (like humans), will choose the most efficient route to travel and indeed, as the tracks indicated, that finger proved to be a veritable highway up the otherwise steep face ahead. We followed it up above the alder belt into a shady Sitka Spruce grove carpeted with moss, as eerily silent and majestic as a great cathedral. The tree growth tapered off before long, becoming stunted at first then disappearing as we neared the alpine.

I was in the lead and halted abruptly when I spotted a bear ahead of us. It was unmistakably a male, in fact, it was a very old trophy-class boar lying alongside of the trail some forty yards to our front, head up, watching us intently. I silently beckoned Brian and Chuck up next to me. We stood there for some time talking quietly and admiring the animal. This was the first grizzly that Chuck had ever seen in the wild, and it was a magnificent specimen for

such an introduction. The bear was of the common (to Kodiak) dark brown color with lighter
blond highlights on his hump and shoulders, an
enormous old boar that would have tipped the
scales at half a ton or better.

The bear presented us with a dilemma. To
get around the animal would be difficult and
time consuming (perhaps impossible) since he
blocked the only reasonable access to the top
of the mountain. He showed no signs of leaving on his own, our presence (apparently) only
a welcome distraction on an otherwise boring
day. We began making noise by shouting, whis-
tling and clapping our hands. The bear reacted by shifting to a more comfortable position
to watch the show, yawning and occasionally
reaching down to scratch his nether regions.
He seemed to find the noise amusing, but only
mildly so. We considered firing our rifles in the
air, but discarded that idea for fear of scaring
off any deer in the area.

I would have paid a lot for a large canister of
pepper spray at that moment... As it was, I was
carrying a Ruger #1 in 7mm Mauser caliber, an
elegant single-shot rifle of Victorian design. I

loved this rifle for its eccentric look and antique quirkiness. The single-shot capability kept me "honest" by forcing me to get in close and make sure of a humane shot since no follow-up was possible. The rifle was also extremely light and handy, not inconsiderable virtues for hunting in the near-vertical Kodiak terrain. Yet, in this case, the rifle seemed more of an affectation than a serious hunting tool as the caliber was well below the minimum one would want to face a brown bear.

The bear appeared to be a mild-tempered old gentleman, so I decided to drive him off, inadequate rifle or not. While Brian and Chuck held back to cover the scene with their rifles, I approached him yelling and waving my hat with one hand and trying to keep my own rifle at the ready with the other. When I got within twenty yards, he simply stood up and walked away, disappearing into the thick brush of the ravine on our left. I was relieved. I expected the bear to do exactly as this one did, but you cannot help fearing that such an action will bring about a threat display or challenge of some sort. This old fellow apparently knew that humans were a nuisance best avoided, and wisely left the scene.

A few minutes climb found us on the barren shoulder of the mountain itself. To our left and south stretched a long level shelf wrapping itself around the mountain until it passed out of sight, while just above us was the rocky crest itself. The ledge was ideal deer habitat offering plenty of cover to bed down during the day, and easy access to the succulent alpine growth just above. It was covered with high grass and interrupted every few hundred yards by little ravines filled with dense alder growth. Patches of grainy snow lay here and there in shaded places. We took a break here to eat some snacks, drink some water and talk strategy. As we chatted, we were entertained by the whales carousing in the bay far below us. We took some pictures of each other against the dramatic backdrop. Eventually, Brian decided he wanted to climb a bit higher and see what lay behind the crest itself. Chuck and I would hunt the ledge while Brian hunted the crags above and tried to keep us in sight.

We had stalked along the ledge several hundred yards when Chuck stopped to take care of something. I do not recall why he stopped - likely to answer a call of nature or dig something out his pack. I continued on another 75 or 100 yards to get beyond a ravine that hosted a tangle of alders and blocked the view ahead. The ravine was perhaps eight or ten feet in depth and twice that in width and had a noisy rushing streamlet cascading over stones in the bottom. I followed a little path down into the ravine (where the sound of the water suddenly became very loud) and continued up the other side until I stepped clear of the alders.

A brown nightmare hurtled from the brush on my left, eyes angry and narrowed, ears flat against the skull, teeth bared.

Chapter 7
The Mauling

The mind has a strange facility for changing the details of past events; even filling in missing information to forever muddy the truth. This is particularly true in moments of great fear and stress, a phenomenon that has embarrassed many a prosecutor when multiple witnesses give varying versions of events. It's been a few years since the mauling and even in that short time I find myself groping for details when I tell the story, or even catch myself "filling in" bits that I don't actually recall. Luckily, I wrote much of this down in great detail during my long convalescence. I suppose I did that as a form of therapy, to put this terrifying event into some sort of context – to put it behind me. It is from those notes that I draw much of the following, the events of November 23rd, 1998.

When I last left the story, I had just stepped clear of the brush to find myself being rushed by an angry sow bear. She was to my left/front at about ten yards and leaping in my direction.

I did not know it at the time, but there was another large male bear just twenty or thirty yards ahead of me to my right front, behind a screen of brush. My friend Brian had just spotted that bear from his vantage several hundred yards above and had been about to shout a warning when the sow erupted from the brush to my left. Brian was too far away to take an off-hand shot at the sow and in any case, she was on me so fast that any shooting from above would have been as likely to skewer me as the bear. He watched helplessly as the bear mauled me, hoping she would draw off long enough for him to risk a shot without hitting me.

The presence of that second bear is interesting. Brian suggested later that this bear was the very same one I had chased from the trail an hour or so before – an extremely large chocolate colored male. Indeed, that bear had gone off to the left to disappear on the hillside somewhere below the ledge in question and could well have managed to find his way up to the location some time before my own arrival. As related elsewhere in the book, sows are enraged by the presence of male bears because of the boars predilection for cannibalizing cubs.

My own actions may have set off a Rube Goldberg-style chain of events that led to my own mauling. I had chased this big male from his comfortable bed and he had blundered into the safety zone of a sow that became frightened and enraged by his presence. I had then silently stalked into the middle of this little wilderness drama from an unexpected direction, only to get a lesson in the law of unintended consequences.

At the time, I was not concerned about how this nightmare had come about. I had other things on my mind, literally; the jaws of an angry sow bear were soon wrapped around my head...

As I relate the following details, you must understand that I had instantly gone into that state of adrenal stress that psychologists have begun to study and quantify in police shootings and military combat situations. The human "fight or flight" reaction has been studied in great detail by a variety of researchers. Some people freeze, some run away, and some do exactly the right thing even when it is contrary to all of the training they have ever had.

When faced with a "fight or flight" situation, the body responds by dumping a number of chemicals into the bloodstream; ACTH, cortisol, aldosterone, vasopressin, histamines, prostaglandins and a dozen other (often poorly understood) chemicals and hormones.

An enormous load of epinephrine creates the first instantaneous (and perhaps most important) reaction by raising the heart and respiratory rate, dilating the pupils (allowing more light to enter) and stimulating the nervous and muscular systems to increase reaction time and strengthen gross motor movements. Simultaneously, there is a release of glucose into the bloodstream to generate extra energy and stamina. Endorphins and enkephalins are released to dampen (or eliminate) pain.

In addition to these clearly useful responses, this chemical soup also produces a number of odd phenomena such as visual exclusion (tunnel vision), auditory exclusion and most oddly; that perception of slowed passage of time so often noted by survivors of traumatic events. While the duration of the mauling was less than a minute in length, it seemed to last a long, long time, and each detail (sometimes even very trivial details) were noted and fixed into my memory, or in some cases bubbled to the surface months later, in my nightmares.

My initial reaction at seeing the bear was to simultaneously raise my rifle and shout at the top of my lungs: "Bear!" "Bear!" The rifle was a new Ruger #1; a very fine single-shot rifle of antique "falling block" design. While elegant and stylish (and perfectly serviceable), the design differed significantly from the standard bolt-action rifle it had replaced; the rifle I had used for many years. I fumbled momentarily before finding the oddly placed safety on top of the tang. I don't mean that as a criticism of Mr. Ruger or his fine rifles, it's just that I've often wondered what would have happened if I'd had my more familiar rifle in my hands? Would I have gotten a shot off in time? It is unlikely, because the rifle wasn't quite up to the level when she hit me, but then, perhaps the fumbling delayed the rise of the rifle to my shoulder? I will never know, and for some reason that bothers me — perhaps because having a rifle in my hands had always imparted a sense of invulnerability, an illusion that was shattered by this event.

I do not actually recall the impact (one of the few details that were lost to me), but it must have been like a drunken taxi driver mowing down an unlucky pedestrian. She simply ran into me and threw me for some yards, knocking the breath out of me and throwing my rifle some yards beyond where I landed. She continued for a short distance, before spinning around and returning to finish me off. I was lying face up, stunned by the impact, when she appeared above me, grabbed my left knee and began shaking me like a dog with a rat. My head and shoulders were being battered against the earth, rocks and alder trunks and it took me a moment to focus on what was happening and react to it – to realize that I was going to die if I did not do *something*! Somehow, I bent forward and hit her on the nose with my fist as hard as I could. It was like striking a tree - and elicited no more response that striking a tree would. I took another swing and my hand was batted aside by her paw. Though I did not note it at the time, one of her claw tips caught me just below the thumb and avulsed most of the muscle and tissue from that area. She followed that up with a swipe at my head, which impacted my right ear and (I learned later) ruptured my eardrum. I raised my right foot as high as I could and brought my boot heel down on her face with all the force I could muster, and this, finally, induced her to let go of me - long enough for me to roll over on my face in the approved "bear safety" position.

As she let go (and before I turned over), some part of my brain noted that her left upper canine tooth was broken off at the tip and split down the middle – an odd example of how very trivial details are filed away only to be recalled much later. In this case, the memory came back to me in a dream many weeks afterwards; I awoke in a cold sweat with a photographically clear picture of her face imprinted in my brain. That picture showed utter fury; the black eyes spitting rage, the teeth yellowed and cracked.

I was now face-down with my hands protecting my vulnerable neck, my torso shielded somewhat by my heavy army surplus "Alice" pack and thinking unkind thoughts about this bear and bears in general. That heavy pack more than any other factor, is probably most responsible for my living through this episode. It became the turtle shell that provided me cover through the terrifying moments to follow. I began yelling as loud as I could for Chuck (who I knew was not far away) to shoot the bear. Perhaps the yelling attracted her to my face because she now grabbed my skull, her upper canines sinking into my right eye socket and cheek respectively, while her lower jaw enveloped the back of my head. The sensation was incredible, as if my head was in a powerful vise.

My vision began to narrow and darken while a roaring sound grew deep inside my head. It was like being under water too long, holding your breath and fighting to get back to the surface, everything beginning to get dark. I remember thinking; "This is it, this is how it all ends..." Yet, as this went on I was also pulling and turning my head away with as much force as I could muster until suddenly it (my head) popped free with a grating sound that I could sense internally rather than hear audibly. Her upper canines had ripped loose from my eye socket and face leaving two furrows from the entry points well into my hairline. I was partially scalped, but she had not "popped" my head, the typical killing method used on deer or moose. My big melon just did not give her the leverage needed to do the job properly.

I buried my face deeper under my arms while the bear reacted angrily by "slapping" me on the back of the head and upper arms. We began a new stage of the game where for some time she proceeded to try and turn me over to get at my face and torso, while I fought her with various stratagems. She would reach under me with a paw or grasp my pack in her jaws and attempt to tip me over while I resisted by using my arms and legs as outriggers or sometimes just doing a "360" by flopping all the way over onto my face before she could pin me on my back. I was assisted somewhat by the fact that I was wedged pretty tightly in some thick alder brush, against which I could find leverage with my arms and legs, while her movements were hindered by that same brush. This went on for some time and at each failure, the bear would angrily punish me for my churlishness in resisting her, with more paw slaps and slashes to my head and limbs.

After a time, she simply dragged me clear of the brush where she could do a more thorough job of taking me apart. She grabbed my upper right arm (her teeth sinking in to the bone) and then swinging me in a semi-circle, dragged me a short distance into the open. I recall my body and legs breaking through heavy branches and then skidding on the ground over a rocky outcropping... and when we stopped I was on my back with her paw on my chest, my arms thrown up to protect my face. She batted at my head and upper arms for a moment as I turned turtle again whereupon she then bit deeply into my thigh and shook me. When I say that, I do not mean she jerked me around on the ground, but she actually picked me up and shook me as the cliché goes "like a terrier with a rat." It was the same bone-jarring shake used by predators to kill or disable small prey. Again, I ripped loose and was on the ground, scrambling desperately to get face down and again screaming for Chuck to "Shoot this bitch!"

She began punishing me again by swiping at me with her paws, her long claws shredding my heavy Gore-Tex jacket and leaving welts on the flesh underneath whenever she happened to miss the pack frame. Most of those hits were claw swipes which did little damage, but I felt a couple of heavy impacts on my back as she threw her weight into several crushing blows that (fortunately) landed on my steel frame pack, dissipating the force enough to protect me to some degree.

This was a beating. I use that term to illustrate something that the word mauling does not imply. The animal is human-like in its general conformation and has the agility of a large human athlete – a sumo wrestler perhaps. A bear mauling involves slapping, stomping, and wrestling if you will, in addition to the obvious bites and claw damage.

She grabbed me by the left buttock and gave me another good shaking. This did not last long - without any bone to grasp in this area, I ripped free almost immediately. She simply grabbed me again near the same spot, repeating the procedure and ripping another goodly amount of flesh away from my upper thigh. Then the pounding and slapping resumed.

People often say brown bears smell bad and so they do when being skinned in the fall after feeding on salmon all summer, since the tissue and fat is impregnated with fishy oils. Yet, externally they just smell like a big dog. I assure you that even her breath was dog-like since afterwards I was covered with her saliva, and could only smell dog and my own blood. Even while it was happening I was conscious of that not unpleasant (to dog lovers) smell that we normally associate with a good-time romp with a playful canine. Why I should take note of that smell during this event is a mystery, but it is one of those small details that I absorbed and still recall.

While all of this was going on, I was experiencing that telescoping time phenomena described earlier. Even though only scant seconds were passing, it all seemed to take an incredibly long time. Most oddly, a part of my brain was actually disassociated from the action as if I was watching all this happen to someone else. While one part of me screamed and fought and raged, the other part watched in resignation, sadly noting the end of my life, wryly amused at such a bizarre demise. I thought about my children, Epi and Connor, wondering what they would think when they heard, what they would do without me. There was a moment of gratification at the realization that I had recently increased my life insurance. My wife could pay off the house and have a large nest egg left over. This may seem incredible and somewhat unlikely, but all of these things were passing calmly through one part of my mind, while another part struggled in the fight for my life.

Then it just ended... At one moment, I was face down in a small patch of snow while she battered me from behind, hitting my head and back with powerful swinging blows and then rising on her hind legs to bring the full force of her weight down on my back through her front paws. Each crushing impact caused me to spit out an unconscious "uh, uh, uh..." I had not heard the shots and I cannot recall them today (auditory exclusion), but I somehow knew that there had been shooting and that the bear was gone.

I was lying face down in sudden peace - a warm and wonderful moment of sheer bliss in the knowledge that the mangling and terror had ended. Someone once said that the single greatest moment in life is to be found in the sudden cessation of great pain. I had not felt any pain yet, but without a doubt, the same truism can be applied to the cessation of great violence and fear.

That happy moment ended abruptly with the realization that I could not see. I suddenly recalled the terrible case of a recent mauling near Juneau where a boy had lost his eyes to a bear.

I had a sinking feeling and a lump formed in my throat as I contemplated a life without sight. I reached up and did a quick exploration with my fingers that revealed that while my right eye seemed to be destroyed, my left felt intact. I blinked and could see a little light and then scraping up a little grainy snow with my hand, wiped my left eye clear to see the world again, a blurry, blood-tinted world, but a welcome sight nonetheless.

As things came into focus, I sat up to find myself in a bloody patch of snow and pulling up another handful, used it to further clear away the blood and debris from around my eyes. I began looking around to confirm that the bear was indeed gone. I recall that Chuck was standing some yards away at the edge of the precipice, looking at me with a shocked expression on his face. My first words to him were a simple and heartfelt: "Thank you." I knew (even at that moment) that it had taken enormous courage and great presence of mind to charge into the carnage.

Another person might have frozen or taken the time to move to some vantage where he could be safe, yet still take a shot at the bear, a delay that surely would have been fatal to me. The bear was rapidly was taking me apart and I could not have lasted much longer. Instead, Chuck moved directly into the scene even though he could not have even seen the bear until he was almost on top of us, past the same screen of brush that had hidden her from me. He could very easily have ended up underneath that bear and I would have been in no shape to help him.

He only nodded at my thanks, and then indicated that he thought the bear was still close by, perhaps hidden in the hillside brush just below us. He had shot it, but did not think it was hurt badly. He turned and began watching the area he had indicated.

I still could not see very well, but I peered around until I spotted my rifle lying some yards away, and began crawling to it. Upon reaching it, I examined it and found the safety in the "off" position. Opening the action I discovered that the rifle was still loaded, the round in the chamber unfired. The moment she had collided with me was then (and still is) a blank spot, but I had not gotten off a shot, a fact I had not known until that moment.

While this was going on Chuck and Brian began shouting back and forth and Brian indicated from his high vantage that he could not see the bear. That was no guarantee of anything as the defilade below the ledge hid much of the hill from his view. I was bleeding pretty badly, but at the moment was more worried about the bear returning than dying of blood loss. Chuck began searching his pack for bandaging materials, but I asked him to wait on that until Brian arrived, reasoning that the bear was the more immediate threat. I crawled onto a slightly elevated patch of ground and laying my rifle across my lap, began taking stock of my injuries.

The most obvious injury was to my head and face, my fingers revealing that a lot of the skin appeared to be gone from around the right side, the eye socket mangled and tattered, the eyelid seemingly ripped away – presumably, the right eye was gone as well. However, I knew that these injuries (even though they were bleeding profusely), were unlikely to kill me. There are no major arteries in the skin of the face.

More troubling was my upper left thigh and buttock which had much deeper wounds and indeed, when I explored the area my entire hand went *into* the flesh in a couple of places – not good and I couldn't tell how badly it was bleeding. I decided the best short-term solution was simply to sit on the injury as a sort of pressure bandage. My upper right arm was also badly mangled, but the wound there was clearly seeping blood rather than pumping it, as would be the case with a torn artery.

My left knee was another bad area. The bear had grasped me there, and dragged and swung me around quite brutally, her teeth ripping the whole area apart. At a glance, you would suppose all of the tendons and delicate structures in this joint were destroyed, yet I was still able to flex it after a fashion, and it wasn't bleeding too badly. At least it wasn't spurting, so again, no arterial damage.

There were numerous smaller bites, bruises and claw lacerations all over my body, but none of them were serious enough to endanger me immediately. I just felt lucky to be alive and my initial examination seemed to indicate that

I might remain so for some time to come. The injuries appeared gruesome but were to some degree superficial. At least there did not seem to be any arterial bleeding or other immediate threats to life. Overall, I was in relatively good shape considering the circumstances.

I could not afford to think past that at the moment, to consider that I was several miles from camp or that the nearest medical facility was forty or so air miles beyond that.

I did not feel any pain and that remained true for the rest of that long day; the injuries were simply *there* without creating any real discomfort. Oddly, my spirits began to soar - undoubtedly, part of that was due to that chemical soup still coursing through my veins, but it was also affected by the sudden realization that (with any luck), I just might survive this after all. We had four or five hours of daylight left and the weather remained clear and calm. There was no reason a helicopter could not make it out here if we could contact the Coast Guard back in Kodiak city. I knew that my friend Ira was back at camp and had a marine band radio among his store of electronic wizardry. The mountains would block any direct contact with town with this line-of-sight radio, but if he could raise *anyone*, they would relay the message on the emergency channel through as many intermediates as was required to get the message to the appropriate people. This is a way of life here and I knew with reasonable certainty that if Ira could raise anyone at all, they would take whatever steps were necessary to get the word passed along. It was just a matter of time. Maybe...

It was about eleven o'clock and the sun would set at about five. Of course, it would fall below the high mountains south of us well before that, and when it did, the temperature was going to drop. It was perhaps twenty-five degrees out, but in the bright sun and nearly windless conditions, it felt much warmer. Yet, when that sun set the temperature was going to drop by perhaps twenty degrees. In the back of my mind I knew that my blood loss was substantial and that when that temperature dropped, the odds of my survival would drop with them.

After some minutes, Brian arrived and while Chuck continued to stand watch, gave me a quick and thorough examination. Digging out clean muslin game bags from our packs, he cut them into strips and soon had the worst injuries neatly contained under some quite effective (if improvised) pressure bandages. Rather than wrap my whole head, he simply covered the right side of my face with muslin and then pulled his own watch cap down over them to hold them in place.

I was carrying several sheets of the reflective plastic foil known as a "Space Blanket" in the small store of emergency supplies that I kept in my pack. This material weighs less than an ounce and can be folded to the size of a wallet, yet has wonderful heat retaining qualities. I dug that out and wrapped it around my legs and lower torso. I also had a small container of ibuprofen and I took several of those, reasoning that even though I felt no pain at the moment, that condition was unlikely to last.

Brian told us that he had observed the entire episode from above the scene. He had just spotted the big male bear ahead of me a few seconds before the sows attack, but had not been overly alarmed because this old fellow had already proved to be genial and obliging. Yet, since I continued along the ledge, it was quickly becoming apparent that I could not see the animal ahead of me. He was about to shout a warning when the sow suddenly appeared from the heavy brush on my left and threw herself on me. The range had been far too great to risk a shot without hitting me, and it had all happened too quickly in any case. He had watched Chuck approach along the ledge and then cross the ravine where he could finally see and take a shot at the bear from the distance of a few yards. At the shot, the big sow had immediately dropped me and charged Chuck who was able to get a second shot off when the bear was only feet away which (apparently) turned her just enough to miss running him down as she had done to me. She was still close enough that Chuck was knocked aside as she passed. He fell to the ground, but quickly recovered and jumped up to discover that the sow had now disappeared beyond some thick alders.

From above, Brian watched the bear travel another 25 yards or so, then turn around and begin heading stealthily back towards Chuck, who could see none of this. Brian steadied up to take a long range shot when suddenly the bear paused as if in thought, then turned aside and went over the brow of the ledge and out of his sight.

From Chuck's perspective, his first inkling of the situation was introduced by my cries for help. He had jogged forward and upon clearing the intervening brush, saw me face down with the bear straddling me, pounding me with her paws and biting at my back. Chuck was carrying a .300 Winchester Magnum loaded with Barnes "X" bullets – a potent rifle and cartridge combination. He was too close to use the scope, so simply "shotgun" sighted along the plane of the barrel and shot the bear somewhere aft of its mid-section (afraid to shoot the "business" end in fear of hitting me). The bear had reacted immediately by turning and lunging in his direction. He had just enough time to jack another shell in the chamber and fire again when the bear was mere feet away. The bear actually knocked him down, but continued in the same direction without stopping to maul him. Perhaps this second shot hit the bear, or it may have been simply stunned by the noise so close to its face, but in any case it changed direction enough to pass him with a glancing blow and then continued into the thicket behind him.

We briefly explored our options. I attempted to stand and walk and (with some support), this proved possible - but blood immediately began to seep through the bandages at an alarming rate. I would be bled dry long before we got back to camp.

Somebody was going to have to run the gauntlet back to camp in hopes of raising help on the radio. I refer to it as a gauntlet because camp was directly downhill several miles to our southeast and the bear had last been seen going in the same direction. Whoever went back to camp was going to have to thread his way through several miles of dense thickets knowing that somewhere within that tangle, a wounded and enraged bear was licking its wounds. Staying with me was no picnic either; we were in a scene of carnage where the angry bear might return at any moment. There was blood splattered in every direction and pools of it on the ground - perhaps that scent would draw additional opportunistic bears to the area.

After a brief discussion (and perhaps because Brian felt he knew the route through the alders better), he elected to go. He left us with all of his survival gear, his water, food, and an additional space blanket and after a quick good bye departed back towards the spur that had brought us up to this place, to begin the long and dangerous trek back to camp.

It is good to have such friends.

The author a few minutes before the mauling

Charles Garwood left, Brian Painter right

The author with Ira Kessler

Aftermath

*The rescue - USCG Flight Corpsman
John Workman*

*The helo in the background is actually
dangerously perched on a ledge*

Chapter 8

Aftermath

It was early afternoon and the weather pleasant, the sun warm on our faces. We were perched there on a ledge, high above a vast tract of pristine wilderness. From our overlook, the southern tip of Uganik Island stretched out in a rough triangle enclosed by the long blue arms of the bay. Across those narrow arms the main island of Kodiak rose to rocky heights to frame the scene in gold and gray. Eagles wheeled on the rising air currents and a pair of whales played in the shallows of a small cove to our west, rolling together and blowing plumes of white mist.

I felt good. I in fact, I can only think of few moments in my life which rivaled this afternoon for sheer enjoyment and appreciation of how good it is to be alive. I am sure part of that mood was chemically induced, a by-product of the chemical soup coursing through my body in response to the recent trauma. Yet, there was more than that going on. There was a psychological high that a death row convict would understand, if reprieved on the morning of his execution. I had been sentenced to death yet, strangely, found myself alive to feel the warm sun and to look out over this lovely vista and appreciate how good life can be.

I dug out a little disposable camera and asked Chuck to take some pictures. I am sure that sounds odd under the circumstances, but I wanted to record the moment. When I look at those pictures now, I do not see the blood or tattered clothing and flesh, I see my goofy grin and that feeling of euphoria comes flooding back.

Life is good!

Chuck was much more concerned about the situation than I was. I suppose that is only natural, since he bore the responsibility to keep me alive. I was just a lump of torn flesh, unable to walk or do anything for myself. Hell, I only had one useful arm and eye! I guess I had more confidence in Chuck than he had in himself. In my eyes, he had already proved that he was courageous and resourceful enough to deal with anything that came up. My life was in his hands and I had no doubts about his ability to handle any new issues that arose.

We talked about the immediate future, calculating how long it might take Brian to reach camp and wondering if Ira could raise anyone on his marine band radio. Such a radio only works on a line of sight basis, making direct contact problematic deep in this bay surrounded as it was by a ring of high mountains. If they could not raise anyone, they would have to climb up the mountain or hike many miles north in hopes of reaching someone at sea. From our vantage, I could see a gap in the mountains directly to the east and I knew that somewhere out there, perhaps 15 miles away, was the village of Port Lyons. It would not take much of a gain in elevation to get a clear shot to the village, but I did not know if they would realize this and there was no way I could tell them now. Surely, Ira was savvy enough to check a topographical map for a good vantage to broadcast from... There was nothing we could do about any of this from up here. It was out of our hands, so we sat back and enjoyed the warm sun.

We estimated that it would take Brian an hour or perhaps an hour and a half, to reach camp. If Ira raised someone immediately on the radio, a Coast Guard chopper could be in the air in a few minutes with a thirty minute run to our location. Therefore (if everything worked perfectly), we might hear the sounds of rotor blades two hours after Brian had departed the scene. We checked our watches and made mental notes.

We calmly discussed the situation. If no help came we would be spending the night here and under this dry arctic air the temperature would drop dramatically after the sun set. The temperature must have been in the single digits in our sea level camp the night before, and doubt-less much colder here on the mountain. Chuck was well dressed, but my clothes were in tatters and I had lost an enormous amount of blood. There was no wood up there aside from a few scrubby alders and we had no shelter except for a few foil space blankets.

Not good.

On the plus side, we had some four or five hours of daylight left, and in this clear weather the Coast Guard could operate at night as well as by day. I knew that my old friend Ira was both resourceful and intelligent. If it were possible to contact anyone, he would be able to do it.

More than once that day (and many times since), I have reflected on how lucky I was to have such friends. Chuck had literally put his life on the line to save me. Brian was doing so at that moment as he traversed the same thickets that had swallowed the angry bear. I had often teased Ira about his love of high-tech gear and now I was counting on that gear and his knowl-edge of it, to get me out of this predicament.

Chuck gathered what little wood was to be found in the area along with some paper, plastic and Styrofoam objects he found in our gear. This little pile would only burn for a few minutes, but he wanted to send up a plume of smoke as a signal when and if we heard an approaching chopper.

There was not much else to be done, so we sat and talked, admired the scenery and told jokes. I am sure if we had had a deck of cards, we would have played a few hands of poker. Chuck would take breaks every few minutes to survey the slope below us for the return of the bear. We had not seen her since she had disappeared over the edge and we were beginning to feel hopeful that she would not return. When she had first attacked me, there had been cubs in the brush behind her. The cubs too had disappeared. I had not seen them since the original rush of the bear, and they had already been gone when Chuck arrived on the scene. I hoped they had also gone down the hill and were reunited with their testy mother somewhere.

In the course of the afternoon, I began to find injuries that I had not noticed before. I discovered that the hearing was gone from my right ear. My right hand did not work correctly and so I finally pulled off my light gloves to discover that much of the tissue was avulsed from the meaty part below the thumb. This was odd because the glove itself was still intact with only a small hole over the rather large injury. I recalled her batting my hand out of the way when I struck her - obviously, the tip of one of her long claws had penetrated like a dagger and hooked out all of this meat. I put the glove back on as a bandage of sorts. I discovered some deep puncture wounds to the back of my head where her lower teeth had grasped me in the attempt to crush my skull. These injuries were relatively minor. More worrisome was the bleeding from upper right arm and left thigh. The thigh and buttock in particular seemed to be seeping blood at a dangerous rate. Chuck added material to these injuries and bound them up a little tighter. He found a little rubber pad of some kind in his pack and I used it as a seat, allowing me to shift more of my weight to the injured side and better stem the blood loss with the direct pressure of my body weight. I avoided examining the eye injury that most troubled me.

I assumed the eye was destroyed because when I had felt the injury after the attack, my fingers encountered naked bone in the socket and over much of that side of my face. Poking around in there with my fingers was liable to eliminate any possibility of repairing the delicate organ, if indeed it could be saved.

Our hopeful two-hour time limit for rescue came and passed without comment from either of us. It was still early afternoon, but the sun was falling ever closer to the mountain crests and the air was taking on a distinct chill. We were quietly chatting when we heard a distinct "bark" from the mountain above us. Kodiak has no wolves or coyotes and we were many miles from the nearest habitation that might harbor a dog; in fact, there were no human habitations at all on Uganik Island. I knew it was a bear. Chuck immediately rose and began scanning the mountain above us, but could see nothing. He suggested it might be a fox, but I knew those animals rarely made sounds - in any case, this sound had been too deep and loud to have come from a tiny fox.

I scooted and crawled as well as I could to a better vantage and began watching the mountain with Chuck. In a few moments, the unmistakable silhouette of a bears head rose from the brush a hundred yards or more above us. It was watching us. I braced my rifle against the ground and fired a shot into the sky, noting with great satisfaction that the animals head had immediately disappeared at the sound. At first, I suspected that this was the sow returning for her cubs, but that notion was quickly dispelled as the head reappeared and then was joined by another, then another... Before long there were four bear heads peering down at us from the mountain. One or two of them began bawling, loudly and repeatedly calling out in pitiful tones of distress – penetrating sounds that would surely carry for miles around.

It was puzzling that there were *four* heads up there. I did not think bears could have that many cubs, but there were certainly four heads up there and they were all of the same size. I had only a glance at the cubs prior to the mauling, but I was certain they were fairly young animals, less than a hundred pounds in any case.

The biologist who later examined the scene told me that four cubs are indeed a rare situation. He opined that a sow with that many cubs would be hard pressed to feed them all, and that this stress was very likely a factor in her temperamental behavior.

The bawling became continuous and much louder as all four of the animals began to cry out in unison. Chuck fired a shot in the air and they quieted for just a moment before resuming their chorus. Worse, one of them began climbing down toward us and was soon followed by the others. They got to within twenty-five or thirty yards and resumed their loud and insistent chorus. We fired more shots in the air and they paid little attention, falling silent for a just a few moments at each shot then continuing to caterwaul at high volume. Chuck picked up some rocks and sticks and approached close enough to begin pelting the frightened animals. This too had little effect - they would retreat a few yards and then return to bawl at him, perhaps even more frightened (and louder) than before.

You must understand that we were not afraid of the cubs; at least not at this point when we could clearly see that they were young animals of seventy-five pounds or so. What we feared was that they would call the angry and injured sow back into the fray. She was still in the area somewhere, presumably injured and as disturbed as when she had attacked me, perhaps even more so since her cubs were not with her. It did not occur to me then, but a biologist later pointed out that the cubs were just as likely to call in any hungry male in the vicinity. The bawling of a young cub is a dinner bell to any boar within earshot.

The cubs were now just above us on the hillside and there was no place for us to go (even if I had been able to walk), except down into the thickets below where presumably, the angry sow still lurked. Even if I could have traveled down into that jungle without quickly bleeding out, we would have then been invisible to any helicopter that came for me.

We continued our efforts to frighten them off with gunshots or thrown objects, with only sporadic success. At times, Chuck would drive them up the hill and they would disappear into the brush and stay silent for short periods, only to return, drawing closer each time. Oddly, they seemed to be bawling at *us* instead of a more general call down the hill, in the direction the sow had departed. I still do not know what that was all about; they were apparently trying to drive us away rather than merely calling for mother.

They finally climbed all the way down onto the ledge with us. They were now fifteen or twenty feet away and still wailing at us.

We began to debate whether we should simply shoot them and be done with it. If the sow was alive, she would surely respond to these cries eventually and neither of us wanted to fight her again. After all, we were armed with deer rifles designed to kill animals a fraction of the size of a mature brown bear, and she could appear from the heavy brush only yards away before we saw her – could we even get a shot off? I doubted I would be much use repelling a charging bear in any case with my right arm and eye out of action.

We were torn between opposing instincts. On the one hand, we did not want to kill these cubs. To do such a thing seemed out of bounds, a violation of the basic precepts of sportsmanship and legality. On the other hand, there was an angry sow out there that eventually would be called in to protect these cubs... Should we put our own lives at risk to spare these young animals?

Perhaps if we shot just one, the others would be driven away?

This episode had been going on for a long time - thirty minutes or more, and she had not yet appeared. Perhaps the sow was dead after all and this was the reason she had not returned in response to these cries? In that case, the cubs would die anyway and a bullet was certainly quicker and more humane than any death Mother Nature had in store for them.

We could not leave, and they would not.

If the sow was alive, she would be called back eventually and we would be forced to kill her or die trying. If she was already dead, it did not matter anyway; the cubs would die without her.

This seemed a logical, if somewhat circular, argument under the circumstances.

Chuck shot the first one. One of them was slightly larger than the others and seemed to lead the way. He (presumably it was a male), was standing on his hind legs upon a little elevation a few yards from us. Chuck shot him in the head and he dropped like a rag doll, unfortunately rolling down the hill closer to us. Instead of running off, the others followed it down and they were now just a few feet from us, still wailing in fear. Chuck shot another one that rolled over, still kicking. I raised my rifle awkwardly to my left shoulder and somehow found the wounded one in my sights and shot it again, killing it. Chuck dispatched the last of them with a single headshot to each and then walked over to make sure they were all dead. They were.

We had silence at last. The sun had dropped to the mountain crests and it was becoming cold. A cold mirrored by the chill in my guts at what we had just done, and at the realization (now that we were free of distraction) that our estimated timeline for rescue was long past.

We were both quiet after that, our optimism sinking with the sun.

In the course of our long wait, we had several times heard the drone of distant aircraft, but as it had been too early to expect rescue we had paid them little mind. I knew too, that aircraft worked on different frequencies than Ira's marine radio, so they were of no consequence at all.

As I learned later, Brian had made good time back to camp and they had begun working the radio immediately. If my understanding is correct, they first made contact with someone in a cabin on the main island. That person began broadcasting on the emergency channel as well as the commercial fisherman's working channel. One of them (either Ira or the homesteader), made contact with a charter boat somewhere nearby who then moved up to the mouth of the bay to get in the clear and relay the message to the Coast Guard.

Back on the mountain, we heard the drone of another aircraft in the distance. By this time, I was beginning to feel pretty weak and lightheaded; clear signs of shock. I was lying back in a semi-reclining position, alone with my thoughts. Chuck suddenly leaped to his feet and began scanning the horizon to the northeast, the direction we expected help to come from. With my damaged hearing, I could not discern anything at first, but before long, I also heard the sound of an aircraft to our northeast.

That sound was electrifying! All my flagging energy and concentration was suddenly refocused. I hauled myself up one elbow and began watching the horizon. Within moments though, it became apparent that the sound was the tenor hum of a single engine plane rather than the deeper bass drone of a helicopter. I sank back to my former position, deflated by the realization. Yet, Chuck remained standing with a hopeful expression on his face and in a few moments I learned why - the sound of a second aircraft was making itself heard as the sound from the first one waned. This one really did have the bass thrum of a helicopter.

Chuck spotted it first, low on the horizon in the direction of town. Try as I might, it was some time before I could see it with my one eye, but when I finally did I could clearly make out the white and red color scheme of a Coast Guard chopper. It swept in above the bay, crossing to a point directly above our camp where it hovered for some time. Undoubtedly, Ira and Brian were indicating to them our position on the mountain from the ground. I remembered our signal fire, and crawled over to ignite the papers and dried grass at its base. I grabbed a silver space blanket and asked Chuck to wave it as a signal.

The aircraft was now moving again, coming directly toward us, then stopping short to make search sweeps lower down the mountain, much to our frustration. The signal fire was soon burning brightly and the plastic and rubber it contained began putting out a sizable plume of black smoke. Chuck was standing on the precipice waving the large foil sheet. Within a short time, somebody on board the helo spotted our signals and the machine began chugging up the face of the steep incline directly toward us.

It hovered above us for a moment, apparently looking for a place to set down - and not incidentally blowing our little burning pile of trash in every direction. I remember thinking

"Great! I've survived a bear mauling only to be cooked in a grass fire..." while Chuck ran around and stomped out bits of burning trash. The helicopter suddenly tilted and made for a place some seventy-five yards along the ledge where it touched down with the entire rear of the machine balanced out over space, the rotor turning to maintain this position.

I suddenly recalled that both of our rifles were loaded and had a mental image of unknown people in the helicopter handling them... disaster. I quickly unloaded mine and shouted to Chuck who followed my lead and emptied his own. People in blue flight suits were now exiting the helicopter and approaching. One of them was now standing over me, shouting something that I could not make out over the sounds of the rotors. He was saying something about the rifle I was holding and I replied that it was unloaded and opened the chamber to show him. He held out his hands for the rifle and I handed it to him, whereupon he pulled a shell from the fabric carrier on the stock and loaded it. I had to grin at that - apparently he was going to keep the bears off while they loaded me aboard.

Another face now leaned over me: John Workman, a longtime friend and a flight medic of vast experience. I was happy to see him and smiled broadly. He just looked at me with concern and shook his head; "Keith, What happened to you?" I just shrugged. He put battle dressings over the muslin bandages (which had soaked through long ago), and got me ready for a transfer in the litter. He also injected me with morphine (which I had at first refused), but then reconsidered, knowing that I would soon have many people poking and prodding at my so far, painless injuries.

The rest was a blur induced by the morphine. They put me in a litter and then suddenly the helicopter was hovering in the sky far above me and I was being hoisted up by cable, before being then dragged into the interior, to safety.

I only have one memory of that flight back to town. I looked around to see Chuck sitting at the rear of the craft and I grabbed John's arm and shouted to him that Chuck had saved my life, that he had risked his own to do it and I wanted the command to know that.

The Coast Guard is a lifesaving service, and months later Chuck was awarded the Meritorious Service Medal for saving my life.

An hour or so later I was in an emergency room having my wounds cleaned and debrided. I recall a nurse poking around in my buttocks finding various leaves, twigs and rocks and getting a great deal of satisfaction at every prize she pulled out: "Look at the size of this rock! How do you suppose that got in there?"

The long process was excruciating. I had felt no pain up until this point, but now that I was safe, it came on in full force. I was entirely conscious for the first part of the process because they needed my participation to survey the damage. I was gratified when they explored my face and pronounced the right eye still intact. Eventually, I was taken into surgery and a very fine surgeon by the name of Dr. John Lundblad was able to repair most of the damage to my face without a lot of scarring, as well as pull everything else back together.

On the following day, I was interviewed at the hospital by our local bear biologist and a state trooper. I told them what had happened and explained why we felt it necessary to shoot the cubs. They then flew into the area trying to find the wounded sow and were able to track her path for some miles and find where she had bedded for the night. She had left a pool of blood there, but upon leaving that scene the bleeding had stopped and they were unable to track her further. The biologist later told me that since the sow had not returned, she had effectively abandoned the cubs and that they would have died or been eaten by a boar anyway. He felt our actions were entirely justified under the circumstances.

So what did I do wrong to put myself in the situation in the first place? If you consider that I was hunting, making noise to warn bears of my approach was not really an option and the bear did not give me an opportunity to back away or de-escalate the situation in some other fashion when we did make contact. I think when all is said and done, if you roll the dice long enough with bears, you are eventually going to have to pay. I was just out of luck that day.

Chapter 9
Bear Protection

I almost wish I could leave this chapter out, but the issue draws so much interest and discussion that it is impossible to write this book without addressing the questions surrounding bear defense.

I do not want to contribute to any general paranoia about bears. I live, hike, fish and hunt around grizzlies and one of my greatest joys is watching and photographing them and other wildlife. Indeed, I would say that in general they are pretty good neighbors... most of the time. It is just as easy to get complacent around bears, as it is to over-react and fear them. Both reactions are extreme. I had certainly grown complacent at the time of my mauling. If you encounter fifty or a hundred bears without a problem, it is easy to get complacent. However, this event was a reminder that you never know what the next one will do. It is a lesson I will never forget again. In the year following my mauling, there were two more attacks right here in my neighborhood, one of them fatal. The animal must be respected and common sense precautions should be taken.

Nobody really knows how many bear attacks occur because there is no central repository for such data. With no great amount of data to draw from, much of the research on the subject relies on anecdotal information, or (at best), very limited sources. In Alaska, we average five to ten bear injuries a year according to newspaper accounts, and perhaps one to two deaths. Many of these injuries are quite serious with people blinded, crippled or disfigured. It happens. People also simply disappear every year out in the Alaskan bush. It is impossible to say how many of these people fell victim to bears, but obviously some of them do.

Before I begin with brown bears, I feel obligated to write a little about black bears. I do not live around black bears and so have little experience with them, but since they are far more common than brown/grizzly bears, the reader is far more likely to encounter them than his larger cousin.

I read somewhere that "black bears are just as dangerous as grizzlies." This is nonsense, but based on a curious bit of factual data; when various deaths attributable to bears are compiled (as subjective and incomplete as those numbers might be); you generally get about an equal number of deaths blamed on each species. That makes the black bear seem quite fearsome, yet if you look at the overall numbers of bears, you will find that there are about 600,000 black bears in North America yet only about 30,000 brown/grizzly bears. Therefore, black bears outnumber grizzly bears by about 20 to 1... Meaning (if the numbers are close to accurate), that you are about twenty times more likely to be attacked when encountering a grizzly than when encountering a black bear.

That does not make black bears safe enough to be taken for granted, but I think we can dial down the paranoia-meter a notch or two in black bear country. Yet, people who know a lot more about black bears than I do, say that one should fight a black bear to his dying breath because if a black gets you down it is almost always about the food. A grizzly will generally swat an intruder down as a way of protecting its "space" and then be content to go on its way, quite indifferent to whether you live or die. You can play dead with a grizzly and have fair odds of surviving the outcome. I am told that with black bears, the opposite is true. If it gets you down, it will usually begin to feed. One should resist a black with a knife, a stick or with fists alone until you drive it off or can no longer fight. To play dead with a black bear is not an option.

Grizzlies and black bears share habitat in many places, but interestingly on the islands of southeast Alaska, the bears are entirely seg-regated. Some islands hold browns and some hold blacks, but none hold both species. Over the years, the browns have simply eaten all the black bears on the islands they inhabit, and being cut off from the mainland no new blacks can wander in from afield to replace them.

That general region also holds a couple of very interesting black bear variants. The Kermode's bear inhabits parts of British Columbia. It is a white "black" bear sometimes called the Spirit Bear, a genetic variant that survives due to the reluctance of natives and later whites, to kill such a unique animal. Further north, through large parts of southeast Alaska up into the general coastal region of Yakutat, one can find the "blue" or Glacier bear, a black bear with a gray/blue coat. This animal evolved along the isolated coast during the last ice age when its coat gave it great camouflage against the icy backdrop. The numbers are declining due to interbreeding with the more common black bears that have moved into the region since the glacial barriers have melted during the last ten thousand years.

Grizzlies also share habitat with the polar bear in their northern range. The polar bear actually descends from the brown bear and at times, these species will mate. The question of whether they mate was debated for years as bears were sighted and killed that seemed to be a cross between the two types. In the last ten years or so at least three wild bears have been DNA tested to validate (finally) that the two ursine cousins do mate. The terms Grolar and Pizzly have been coined to describe such crosses, a Grolar having a grizzly male and polar female parentage, while the Pizzly is born of a grizzly female and a polar male.

One indicator of just how many problems occur with bears in Alaska is the number of hides sold by the state each winter after being turned in by those who shoot a bear in "Defense of Life or Property" (DLP). The number of DLP hides varies year by year, but I note that in 2009 there were 117 such hides sold. No doubt, many of those bears were simply nuisance bears killed while raiding chicken coops or stock pens, but that's an awful lot of bears killed in a state with such a small human population. Most of those hides (presumably) are from bears killed in legitimate self-defense.

Most of the time there is no apparent reason for an attack and by this; I mean most of the victims are not an obvious threat to the animal. Bears simply attack because they are bears. They fight among themselves and are intelligent enough to be moody and angry for some days after a fight. A bear who has just lost a fight might very well take a swipe at the next mammal it runs across, perhaps you. Bears are frequently injured in these fights, breaking teeth and receiving other injuries that plague them for months and years. One can only speculate *why* a particular bear attacks someone.

Some outdoor activities put people at higher risk than others. In particular, I am thinking of joggers here. When you run from a predator, you are inviting that prey/predator response that biologists talk about. Just like the mean dog you came across when you were a kid that chased you when you ran away, running also invites bears to chase you. If you run you are prey in the eyes of a bear, and that is what joggers do – they run. Compound that with the tendency of joggers to plug an IPod or some other music device in their ears and you have a real potential for disaster. Runners are often completely unaware of their surroundings and any audible clue from the animal that might alert them to turn and face the threat is hidden behind the music. A few years ago right in the city of Anchorage several people jogging in parks were taken down through the course of a single summer. Only a year or two ago, a young schoolteacher freshly arrived from the lower 48 was killed by a pack of wolves while jogging outside a village on the mainland opposite Kodiak. These types of attacks are a frequent pattern, so much so that it is becoming a very common scenario for summer bear attacks. Luckily, most of these are of the "swat and run" variety – the animal simply knocks the jogger down, takes a couple of swipes and bites then moves on after administering a lesson.

I think it is a very bad idea to jog in any area where large predators are present! If you read any of those little pamphlets put out by wildlife agencies, they all have one thing in common; they advise you never to run from a grizzly, so why go out and deliberately run from them? It is not a form of entertainment that I would recommend, and it is certainly not conducive to good health in bear country. An analogy might be running in a large metropolitan area. There are certainly places that invite running as well as bad areas of town you would not choose because of the potential of a mugging. If you choose to run near wild predators, you are just as liable to be "mugged." I might also add here that mountain bikers frequently run into trouble with bears. It might be a good idea to drape your bike with a couple of bells, and again, it is certainly a bad idea to block your hearing with a music device while riding in wilderness areas.

Hunting is a particularly dangerous activity in grizzly country. Everything the hunter does in his silent approach into the wind to stalk a moose or other game animal can also bring him into unseen proximity to a bear. Add to this the likelihood that the bear is lying up in cover deliberately hiding, perhaps in an ambush position on a game trail – a game trail that a silent hunter might be following... Moreover, hunting season is in the fall when bears are in hyperphagia; desperate to seek out every morsel of fat and protein it can get before hibernation.

They are cranky and stressed and in no mood to be genial to any bipeds they run across. If the hunter bags his deer or elk, he has now released the scent of blood into the air, a smell that can draw bears from miles away. Make no mistake, rifle shots mean gut piles to bears. They will investigate and they will sometimes challenge a hunter for his kill. More often, problems develop after a hunter leaves his kill for a time and returns to find it has been claimed by a bear.

If you hunt in grizzly country, you need to have a partner. If you get a large animal down that cannot be packed out immediately, it needs to be quartered and suspended in a tree. That is still no guarantee that a bear will not be waiting for you when you return, so you should assume the worst and be ready to deal with it. A wise approach might be to have one person wielding some pepper spray while one or more others have rifles to back that up.

Dogs and bears are another dangerous combination. It is not unknown for some small dog to chase a bear across hill and dale, yapping at its heels. Of course, it is also not uncommon for a dog to begin harassing a bear only to have the animal turn and chase the dog, sometimes right back to the owner! Still, bears do seem to have an innate fear of dogs. I do not know if that is some genetic pass-me-down after thousands of generations of competing with wolves, or simply that they associate dogs with humans and thus view them as an animal best avoided.

Bears and dogs are related, or at least descend from the same raccoon-like ancestors. Dogs seem to react strongly to bears, perhaps viewing them as some sort of strange uber-canine. A couple of years ago on a sunny summer morning I was watching a bear in the creek near my house. This bear was about fifty yards off the main road and before long; a woman with a small lap dog of some kind stopped her car nearby and got out to take a picture. The little dog also jumped out and immediately ran down to the creek, happily yapping at the bear and wagging its tail. I cringed; fully expecting to see the dog scooped up and eaten like a hairy salmon, but the bear merely watched the dog for a few moments and then began walking downstream to find a more peaceful place to fish. At this, the little dog simply turned and went back to its somewhat frantic owner.

That story is as typical of such encounters as any, but dogs and bears can be a volatile mix at times. I am reminded of a story told me by a park service employee of a couple walking their dog on a trail in southeast Alaska. The dog ranged ahead to encounter a black bear and immediately began worrying the animal and chasing it. The bear did not run far, but turned and chased the dog right back to the owners who suffered some serious bites and swipes in the resulting melee. Luckily, the encounter did not last long and both the victims were able to get back to their vehicle and thence to the hospital under their own power. The dog was apparently waiting at the vehicle, delighted at the exciting morning it had experienced.

If your dog is not well disciplined, you should probably think very hard before taking the animal where it might come in contact with bears. On the other hand, a disciplined and well-trained dog can be a warning system or even intervene to save you.

It is also worth pointing out that bears are enough like dogs that the same mannerisms, postures and vocal commands that seem to work on dogs will often work on bears. Those who live in rural areas where dogs are often un-leashed and "on guard" will better understand that your reaction to the dog has everything to do with how your encounter turns out. If you are firm but unthreatening, you are unlikely to be bit. If you are hesitant and fearful or run from the dog, you may be in trouble. It is much the same with bears.

One thing I have learned is that very few people really grasp *how* bear attacks occur. If you take anything from this book, please absorb the following pages. I am going to talk about brown/grizzly bears here, because those are the bears I know best. Black bear attacks (I am giv-en to understand) generally unfold quite differ-ently, but browns follow a definite pattern. The attack of a brown bear is almost always sudden and without warning.

There are predatory attacks when the animal wants you as protein, but these are relatively rare. Most often, it is what I term the "surprise" attack, where the victim inadvertently gets too close and invades a bear's space. In either case, the pattern is quite similar.

In a predatory attack, it will stalk up quietly and then rush you from close range. By close range, I mean well under fifty yards, perhaps as close as ten yards – the range depending on available cover, and how close it can get without being detected.

The surprise attacks are much the same, except that the animal is not deliberately stalking you, but feels its space has been invaded and for whatever reason decides to maul the interloper rather than flee. It is lying in the brush (perhaps sleeping), when somebody walks up on it. The theory is that these attacks are an ingrained response to other bears. Bears are not territorial in the biological sense of the term, meaning that they do not have a fixed zone of land that they claim as their own. Nevertheless, they certainly have a space around themselves that will provoke a reaction if invaded. The size of the space and the type of reaction varies greatly and is wholly unpredictable. The bear may rise and exhibit a threat display, it may flee or it may simply rush and attempt to kill or maim the interloper.

In July 2011, a group of seven teenagers came to Alaska for a thirty-day wilderness education course. Near the end of their adventure, they were crossing a stream when they were attacked by a brown bear. The school taught all the recommended bear avoidance techniques. These kids had bells on their gear and were talking loudly and doing all the right things, yet despite all this the noise of the water and wind allowed them to get close to a bear without either party being aware of the other. The animal simply rushed from cover and began taking kids down, seriously injuring four of them.

This was in every way typical of a brown/grizzly attack. There was no warning, the bear rushed them from close range and went right through the group. These kids had bear spray, but none of them had time to employ it before the bear was among them. What is interesting is the statement the instructor made to the press after the attack:

"The bear came really fast, that's what was super unusual."

The instructor, a supposed expert, thought it **unusual** that the attack was so sudden! If you take anything from this chapter, absorb the fact that these attacks usually happen as described above and not as described in fiction novels or Hollywood movies. The grizzly is not going to stand on its hind legs one hundred yards away and roar for a while, then lumber slowly at you while you climb a convenient tree. That is never how it happens outside of Hollywood. Typically, your only warning is the sound of a heavy animal running or breaking brush from a range of less than 20 yards.

Bears are ambush predators and that is how an ambush is executed. It is important to know how these attacks unfold if you are going into grizzly country. It makes no sense to be ready for the Hollywood bear attack when the reality is so very different.

Agencies often fall back on half-truth when putting out information on grizzlies for the general public, repeating a sort of "rote" memorization of facts that ignores the diverse nature of the animal. One of the problems is that they tend to apply facts garnered from a study in one region to bears in another or even one species to another. This is a mistake. It ignores one of the most basic truths about the bear, the enormous adaptability of the species throughout its range. You will often see biological information on diet, seasonal or predatory habits (even very basic data like size and color) that have almost no applicability at all outside of the area where the facts were gathered. A grizzly in Montana does not act (or even look) much like a grizzly in Kodiak. They do not eat the same foods and they do not have the same nature or habits or seasonal movements. All of this can be very misleading and dangerous if you are relying on this information to guide you in some wilderness activity.

An example of poor understanding was illuminated by a recent bear fatality involving a geologist in late winter on the Kenai Peninsula - surely somebody in authority relied on the biological "fact" that bears hibernate through the winter when making the decision to allow dozens of noisy, unprotected workers to tramp around prime bear habitat in coastal Alaska in February. Surely it is true that bears *do* stay in the den in Wyoming or central Alaska (or wherever a particular study was done), but this does not apply in mild coastal Alaska where bears frequently exit the den in winter or sometimes do not hibernate at all. One of these geologists was killed by a brown bear and might not have died had he and his colleagues been armed with firearms or pepper spray – something they thought they would not need at that time of year. Bad information leads to bad decisions and there is a lot of bad information out there.

One of the key bits of information that is often overlooked is that bears are far more dangerous in spring and fall than in summer. They are simply hungry and bad tempered in those seasons. I give bears a much wider space in those hungry seasons than I do in summer when they are fat and happy. I am not suggesting brown bears commonly attack people to eat them (though, they sometimes do...), it is just that hungry bears are foul tempered bears.

This seasonal difference is a lesson that the late Timothy Treadwell would have done well to absorb. He made a remarkable series of films of summer bears in Katmai Park. The animals were friendly and tolerant of him over several seasons, allowing him to approach and film them from close range during the summer salmon glut. Yet, the very first time he went in after the salmon runs had collapsed, in October, his furry pals killed and ate him and his companion.

One of the problems (I think) with getting good information is that while biology has a good grasp of these diverse issues, they are forced to reduce all of this to its lowest common denominator to fit into the small pamphlets and informational booklets provided to the general public. Most of the information in these sources is good – avoidance is indeed the best tactic and this is widely covered and done quite well. Yet, rarely covered are the tactics to be employed when avoidance fails. Should they advise people to carry firearms or pepper sprays? Are they liable if they recommend use of a product and it fails?

In addition to the legalities involved, there is certainly an element of political correctness at work here. How does a government entity (which is after all, the steward of our wildlife) sound when it advises you to shoot a bear in this or that circumstance?

Wherever the blame lies, it is difficult for people to get the information they need. I hope the information in this book is helpful, but it was never intended to be a general lesson plan for hikers or campers in bear country, and in any case deals almost entirely with coastal brown bears which represent only one small sub-species in North America. I cannot tell you what you need to know about bears where you live, but I advise you to learn what you can from local sources.

The odds of a problem are low in most places since most places simply do not hold many bears. Even where bears are numerous, you might run across a hundred grizzlies before running across one with an attitude. Many people, even in grizzly country, may not see one in their entire lives. Bears are secretive and largely nocturnal in areas where people are present.

The odds are worse in places like coastal Alaska since population densities are as high as one grizzly per square mile. Yet, even here, a bear attack is a relatively unusual event.

The more you know about bears, the less likely you are to have a problem. Very few bears are a threat to humans and quite often the bear that appears to be a threat is not at all. A good example is the classic threat display whereupon the bear puts on a show; puffing up, chuffing, clicking teeth, pounding the ground and so on. This is not an attack or even a prelude to an attack. It simply means you are too close. Such displays will nearly always play out peacefully if you simply back away or allow the bear to back away. If you were to shoot in such a situation, you might precipitate the very mauling you are trying to avoid. A bear's brain is the size of a softball and piercing that brain or the spinal cord is the only sure way to stop the bear on the spot. A shot to the chest, shoulder, etc, might kill the bear, but a bear that bleeds out and dies ten minutes after you shoot it, is not going to increase your odds of survival. A bear, especially an adrenalized bear in attack mode, is a tough animal to kill and an even tougher animal to kill on the spot.

Should you carry a gun in bear country?

Yes, I think you should, if you are well trained with firearms. When all is said done it is not the odds, it is the stakes. If you are not comfortable with guns, then you should carry pepper spray or ideally, both. By pepper spray, I do not mean the tiny cans that women carry in their purse, but the large commercial spray sold in sporting goods stores for bears. The spray has a lot more applications than a firearm. You can squirt any bear that comes near whether it is a real threat or not. Pepper spray is good for bears, since it teaches them to avoid humans. Bears that avoid humans live longer than bears that do not.

I want you to think of the following advice on firearms as a last resort measure. You have already taken all the normal preventive measures; your camp is clean, your food is sealed in containers, you are doing your cooking well away from your camp and you are cleaning and storing your fish or meat well away from camp.

You have pepper spray for nuisance bears around camp.

These measures will normally keep you from having bear problems around your camp, but that is not where most attacks happen. Most actual attacks happen as a simple consequence of surprising a bear on the trail, so that old adage about making noise or attaching bear bells to your clothing is good advice. Of course, if you are hunting, you cannot do that, and even if you are not hunting, there are places where those sounds are covered up by loud streams or other natural noises. If you awaken a bear they will generally move away from you, but sometimes they do not and there is no rhyme or reason to it. At the risk of repeating myself, the grizzly may simply rush the animal (you) that has invaded its space. There is none of the TV drama you would expect – they do not roar, they do not stand up on their hind legs, they do not telegraph their intentions in any way. They simply rush you from short range at speeds that top out at 35 miles per hour. You will have one to two seconds at most to realize what is happening and employ your pepper spray or firearm.

Often, that is where everything goes wrong.

If you have pepper spray, it is most likely in a pocket on your pack and you have to get it out, pop the safety tab and then squirt the bear in the face. Pepper spray is great stuff for that problem bear around camp, but in an actual attack, it is slow to get into action. If you do somehow manage to get it employed in time, it is a pretty good defense. It has been successfully used on any number of occasions and is close to 100% effective in stopping bears. If you are going to rely on pepper spray, you had better have it in a place that is instantly accessible. It will do you no good at all if carried in a compartment of your pack. UDAP is one company I know of that markets bear spray with a handy chest holster made of nylon or some similar fabric. It fits over your outer clothing and puts the spray on your chest where it is easily accessible. The founder of the company survived a grizzly mauling, which is what prompted him to create the product and the easily accessible chest holster to carry it. Make no mistake, pepper spray is extremely effective on bears, but like any weapon it has to be employed *right now* and quite obviously, the man behind this company "gets it." They have a website. Google is your friend.

What about handguns? Well, a magnum handgun can certainly kill a bear, but you run into some of the same time constraints as with the pepper spray. Yet, it is worse because even if you get it drawn and leveled in time you still have to hit an object little bigger than a soft-ball (the bear's brain) for a guaranteed "stop." Moreover, that hit has to be done on an animal bounding in your direction at high speed. A hit in a place other than the brain or spine may turn the animal or it may not. Honestly, I would feel much better protected with pepper spray than any handgun. If you get the spray going, you have better odds of turning that animal than with a handgun. I will not argue with anyone who thinks a big bore handgun is a good choice for brown bear country. There are plenty of people better than me with a handgun, but let us consider a couple of points surrounding the issue of handguns. First, a bear's brain is about the size of a softball and hitting that brain is the only guaranteed "stop" when things go wrong. That brain is coming at you somewhere in excess of 30 miles per hour and it's not coming in a straight line, but bounding over the ground in an up and down pattern. If somebody were to stand 25 yards away from you and bounce a softball along the ground at the same speed, could you draw and hit it with your handgun before it reached you? I certainly could not, at least not with any consistency.

Of course, that's not an easy shot with a rifle or shotgun either, but if you miss that shot with either of these weapons, you still have a much greater chance of hitting that animal in the torso with enough energy to put him down, even if it's only a temporary situation that gives you a second shot. A shotgun slug or rifle in the 30.06 class or greater has much more energy than a .44 magnum handgun so the odds rise dramatically in your favor. Of course, the .44 is no longer the big boy of the handgun world, but even with the big .500, you are still at an accuracy disadvantage when considering that all-important central nervous system shot. You may only get one shot!

So, where do you place that shot? There is an old myth about the head of a bear being bulletproof. The story variously goes that because of the thickness or angle of the cranial vault, bullets will somehow ricochet off leaving the bear magically unharmed. It isn't true. The genesis of this old tale is due to a complete misunderstanding of basic bear anatomy. A bear's brain is simply not located where many people think it is. Bears (in particular the grizzly) have a prominent forehead, yet all of that space above the level of the eyes is due to a bony crest which serves as the attachment for various jaw and neck muscles. A bullet going into that space is not going to hit the brain or anything else very important.

The brain is actually an oblong affair lying low in the head with the very top roughly at the level of the eyes and then running down and back from that point. Therefore, if forced to shoot a bear in defense with (presumably) the face pointed directly at you, the ideal aiming point is through the nose because a shot there will center the brain. The nose, being a somewhat prominent landmark, makes a good aiming point so you might as well try for that shot. Of course, making the shot is problematic when considering the rapid movement of an attacking animal coupled with your own fear and stress, yet since the animal is going to be coming in with his head held low and roughly centered in the rest of the torso, even a miss might do the trick. A high shot may very well spine the animal, a miss left or right might take out a shoulder.

The typical hunting rifle certainly has all the power and penetration needed to dispatch a large bear. Yet, something I have learned over my years of deer hunting in Kodiak is that the typical sporting rifle mounted with something like a 3x9 scope is very nearly useless at close range. That magnification and narrowed field of view makes you nearly blind at any distance that could conceivably be thought of as self-defense range for bears. If you are going to hunt in bear country, use iron sights or something like a 1x5 or 1x4 scope kept at 1x until you need to take a long shot. A good lever action in .45/70 along the lines of the Marlin Guide Gun is both handy and powerful enough for any situation.

In the early 1960's Remington Arms went to various bear guides in coastal Alaska and

solicited input for a new rifle specifically designed for bear hunting guides. The recom-
mendations they received were somewhat
surprising and the rifle they designed (and
the new cartridge designed to be shot from it)
was quite odd when compared to the standard
hunting rifles of the day. That rifle and the cartridge have become almost iconic in Alaska, but
are little known anywhere else, the Remington
Model 600 and the .350 Remington Magnum
cartridge.

For those not overly familiar with bolt-action rifles, the actions are made in three different lengths; a long action for cartridges like
.375 H&H magnum, a standard action for cartridges like the 30.06 and a short action for cartridges like the .308 or .223. Well, these bear
guides wanted a magnum cartridge in a short
action, which is quite a tall order (pun not intended...). The reasons for that were that their
worst nightmare was rooting out wounded
bears from the thick alder jungles they tended
to head into when wounded by an inept client.
A short action means the rifle overall is shorter
and lighter, thus easier to swing around in the

thick brush and the shorter bolt throw means that can follow-up shots can be delivered quicker. In addition, they wanted a heavy bullet at high velocity to convincingly put the lights out on any bear they encountered.

The Model 600 delivered all of that. When it was released in 1962, it had an eighteen-inch barrel, topped with a rib sight not unlike a shotgun for instinctive shooting. The short and stubby .350 Remington Magnum cartridge could deliver a 250-grain bullet at 2,600 feet per second. It was a heavy hitter in a short little carbine package. Unfortunately, as popular as these rifles were in Alaska, they were a failure everywhere else. Hunters just did not want or need such a rifle in the lower 48, so due to low sales Remington stopped making them in the late 1960's.

After the mauling, I decided that if I was going to continue to hunt deer on Kodiak Island, I would be smart to get a rifle that could deal with bears as well. I searched long and hard for an old Model 600, but in Alaska, these iconic rifles are snapped up immediately when they become available and I was never able to procure one.

After a time, I contacted the Remington Custom Shop and had them build a .350 Remington Magnum in a Model 7 (short action) package with a sturdy set of iron sights. When I received it, I installed a Burris 1x5 scope with a quick-detachable mount. This rifle has served me well. It is light and handy for packing and gives me reasonable range for deer hunting – 250 yards or so. Ammo is difficult to find, so I reload my own. I think this is a reasonable compromise rifle for hunting in Alaska. Yet, really, anything in the 30.06 class or up will serve. I would just advise (again) that no matter the rifle, the hunter in Alaska needs a scope that dials down to 1X. If things go wrong, it will be extremely sudden and happen at very close range.

Shotguns, loaded with slugs, are the traditional choice of those wildlife professionals who must find and dispatch problem bears. A shotgun slug has plenty of power and penetration, but more importantly, a shotgun is designed for rapid and instinctive point shooting. The same weapon that can be swung up to shoot pheasants or clays with birdshot can be swung up just as quickly to throw a slug at a rushing bear. If you are fishing or camping in bear country, a short-barreled pump shotgun is probably the best all-around choice of firearm. Most shotguns have fixed sights, so I would caution you to make sure yours shoots to point of aim with the ammo you choose. It is not a good idea to choose the hottest magnum sabot slug, if that slug shoots a foot high when you actually need it. Try out different slugs and choose the one that hits where your gun points. Accuracy trumps ballistics.

If you shoot a bear, there will be an inquiry. If it is legitimate self-defense, then you will not have a problem. If it is not legitimate, you may find yourself in some very troublesome and expensive legal proceedings.

If the grizzly is running at you, shoot it. If not, back away. That is about as succinct as I can make it.

Chapter 10
Getting over it

The winter of 1998/99 was another exceptionally cold and bleak one. It was the second bad winter in a row that we had had to endure, and nearly as bad as the previous year which had broken many records for sustained cold. The normally soggy winter landscape of Kodiak was covered in deep snow for much of the winter and spring, and every time the weather began to warm and melt off this white blanket, we would get an arctic cold front to freeze the wet snow into impenetrable concrete-like slabs. It was a calamity for the deer herds with winter mortality estimates ranging as high as 70% in some areas. The cold also locked up the winter moisture, exposing streambeds for long periods and killing untold numbers of salmon lying encased in eggs under the (now) frozen gravel beds.

I did not get out much through that long winter and spring. I recall going out rabbit hunting on one occasion, but the miserable frozen terrain aggravated my still-healing injuries while the few rabbits I saw were skinny and starving, reduced to gnawing alder bark to survive. It probably would have been a kindness, but I did not have the heart to shoot any of them – they were hardly edible in their present condition in any case.

It was not until the following July that I began to get out in the bush again. I began fishing, hiking up into my favorite salmon holes, only now carrying a .45/70 lever gun along with my fishing rod. This was something I had never felt the need to do in the past when fishing near town, where the bears are "educated" to human contact. I was not out of place; in fact, even along the relatively tame streams of the Kodiak road system, there are plenty of bears and most people carry some sort of firearm whenever they left the crowded fishing holes along the road itself. Yet, I had never felt the need to do so and it made me feel a little foolish.

I did not see any bears on my fishing trips, though the tracks were evident everywhere along the streams. The shy road system bears are almost entirely nocturnal and in fact, I did not see another bear until late summer when I took my son Connor out for some deer hunting. We have a favorite deer hunting spot, a secret place where we have gone hunting together since he was only six years old. Our special place is a long ridge that snakes up into the alpine country in gradual stages, a route that Connor could negotiate even when he was very young. He was eight now, and our annual late summer hunt had become a tradition that we both looked forward to. I knew that the odds of bagging a deer were slim after the preceding winters had reduced the herds, but it was the hunt itself that mattered, that and the time we spent together on these little father/son adventures.

When hunting near home I often brought George along, equipped with a load bearing pack. The wolf enjoyed these excursions tremendously, and would proudly pack as much as 50 pounds of meat down off the mountain. She was a wonderful old girl and a great companion on fishing and hunting trips. I should explain that she was indeed a wolf; one of those animals that are usually referred to (euphemistically) as a "high percentage wolf-hybrid" for various legal reasons, yet I doubt very much that there were any dogs in George's family tree. You cannot raise such an animal as you would a dog because these animals do not recognize human authority in the way a dog does. Instead, you have to integrate them into your family until they bond as a "pack member" and become obedient because they choose to follow the rules of the pack rather than for reward or fear of admonishment. Done correctly, these animals are a joy to be around, far smarter than dogs, gentle and obedient – or, at least obedient in those things the wolf finds important... Anyway, as

I've pointed out earlier, she was a sort of "radar" for bears, able to sense their presence at incredible distances.

George was more of a friend than a pet. I used to brew my own beer back in those days and George liked a bowl or two upon occasion. Her favorite was a dark and malty Scotch Ale that I also favored. For a long time after the mauling, I was under a lot of stress and had trouble sleeping. Sometimes I would get up in the middle of the night and pour myself a beer. George would show up and drop her bowl at my feet indicating she wanted to join me. I would pour her some and she'd enjoy slurping it up and making various throaty commentaries about life in general, much of which, like baths, displeased her. The more she'd slurp, the more commentary she had and the louder it became, so sometimes I'd have to cut her off after two or three bowls, but by then I'd also be ready to be cut off so we'd both go back to bed feeling better after sharing our burdens.

Wolves have amazing dexterity with their paws. The paws are like snowshoes that spread out much further than a domestic canine and they learn how to use them almost like a human hand. For example, she figured out how to open doorknobs at a very young age. She'd just stand up and grasp it with both paws, give it a turn and be gone for hours visiting her various dog friends and finding smelly things to roll in. One time I returned from a caribou hunt with several hundred pounds of boned out meat divided roughly into fifty-pound bags or pack loads. I put these bags in an outdoor shed overnight and failed to lock it. When I got up in the morning, George was sleeping in the sun on the back porch with her belly bloated beyond recognition. She had let herself out of the house and thence into the shed to eat almost an entire fifty-pound bag of meat! This is pretty much the normal wolf pattern of feast and famine, but I woke her and told her in no uncertain terms that she was a bad, bad wolf. She did not seem very concerned about it, and went right back to sleep.

Connor, George and I climbed up our favorite ridge in the early dawn of a beautiful late summer day, pausing at each high knoll to glass the saddles ahead. It was misty at first, but as the sun rose and began to warm the air, the fog began to fall and reveal a cloudless summer sky. Soon, only the peaks stood like so many emerald green islands awash in a milky sea. We paused on a knoll to take in the sight and were treated to a breathtaking phenomenon: the light breeze was pushing a fog bank through a low saddle in the ridge ahead of us and it was pouring down the steep slopes on the far side like an enormous waterfall to cascade into the pool of fog already collected in the valley on the far side. It was an incredible thing to see, a sight that made the long climb worthwhile even if we did not find a single deer. It was a very fleeting thing, lasting only a few minutes before the warming sun burned it all away.

We rose and continued along the ridge ever higher into the alpine, without seeing a single deer. We were enjoying ourselves nonetheless, chatting quietly and discussing the things that an eight year old finds fascinating in such a place. George was staying very close to us, as was her instinctive habit when she knew we were hunting. She was no use at all in finding deer; she simply ignored them as she had been taught when young.

We had crested a ridge and began descending the other side when George suddenly threw herself against my knees in a painful fashion. Her neck fur was bristled up and she let out a throaty moan to alert me that a bear was nearby. She was focused on the game trail at our feet and her excitement told me that the trail was very fresh; the bear very close indeed. We were down a steep rise with rocky pinnacles looming over us from both sides. My first instinct was to swing around and make sure we had not simply bumped the bear off the trail and onto the heights above or behind us. Our immediate surroundings were clear, offering no hiding place for lurking bears. Immediately ahead of us the trail descended into a saddle (in fact the saddle that had hosted our ethereal waterfall not long before) and then rose again to the next peak, a half mile or so ahead. On that trail, at a distance of several hundred yards, I saw a bear moving quickly, almost running, away from us. It was moving so quickly that it cleared the next ridge and went out of sight before I could even point it out to Connor.

It frightened me. Clearly, this bear was departing the area at high speed to avoid us, yet I did not want to take another step down the trail in that direction. I knew, intellectually, that there was nothing to fear, yet that knowledge did not take the cold chill out of my guts. I was defeated by the mere sight of a bear and led the way homeward, rather than walk those sunny ridges with my son.

That was a sad moment. I could not help but wonder if this was a precursor to life from now on; a life robbed of the sweetness of the wilderness around me. Yet, it turned out that this wasn't the case The next bear I saw didn't take the wind out of me nearly as much, and every one after that became easier.

In November of the year following my mauling, a man named Ned Rasmussen was hunting deer on the mountain dominating the southern tip of Uganik Island, the same location where my little adventure had occurred. He shot a deer and his companions left him to butcher and pack it out. He never came back to camp. He was later found dead, killed by a bear. Because of the location, I am convinced Rasmussen was killed by the same bear that attacked me. There is no way to prove that, but given the location and time of year (bears return to the same denning area each November), I am sure in my own mind that it was her. She certainly had reason to dislike humans after her encounter with me...

The state went through the usual show of looking for the offending bear, but nothing was found. On the other hand, perhaps, if truth be told, there is simply no way to tell which bear in a given area has done the deed. I like to think she is still out there and that she has had more cubs to replace those we killed. I am not aware of any further attacks on Uganik, so I suspect she either is dead or has mellowed.

I have made a few bear friends over the years. One pair of youngsters in particular have captivated my interest in the last four or five years. Several streams empty into the bay near my home some miles outside of town. One year a sow showed up with a pair of three-year-old cubs and I would see them as I left for work at 5:00 or 5:30 in the morning. I got in the habit of leaving early on clear days to watch and photograph them learning how to fish. There was a young male that I nicknamed Blondie and his very dark and slightly smaller sister that I nicknamed Blackie, because I am really not very clever. The sow kicked them loose early in the season and the pair stayed together through that first summer. I did not think they would make it through their first winter because neither of them seemed particularly skilled at fishing and they remained skinny and gangling. They were clumsy and so inept that they rarely caught a fish and often relied on picking apart the scraps other bears left behind. One day Blondie carried a small humpy salmon ashore and I watched sadly bemused as an eagle swooped in and stole the fish. The big raptor landed on a snag and picked the fish apart while Blondie circled him warily. Eventually, the eagle carried his prize out of sight and left the young blond bear hungry and forlorn at the mouth of the stream.

The larger bears fishing the same streams would chase the young pair away from the prime fishing spots. The hungry duo would hang back and occasionally dash in to pick up any scraps left by the adults. Most of the big bears could filet a salmon almost as cleanly as a human, stripping the meat away to leave the head and backbone for the pair to run away with. When the run was particularly heavy, some of the more epicurean bears would just eat the egg sacks and leave most of the flesh intact for our intrepid young pair. By the end of the summer, the pair had filled out and become somewhat glossy, if not fat like the older bears. At some point, Blackie was badly wounded in her buttock. I noticed one day that she was limping and had an angry wound that looked as if a larger bear had taken a chunk out of her. That wound healed, but would help me identify her in succeeding years because it left a whitish patch on her rump. Her brother was easy to identify because of his rare (for Kodiak) blond color. That first year is always rough for young bears kicked loose by the sow, but watching this pair really brought that fact home to me.

The following July they returned with the pink (humpy) salmon run and made great strides in learning to catch fish. They still ran together much of the time early in the season, but they developed very different fishing styles. Blondie used the typical method of chasing the salmon into the shallows of the stream and leaping on one. However, Blackie developed a technique I have never seen any other bear use. She'd come down to the bay at high tide and swim around in the brackish pools surrounded by salt marsh, diving underwater and frequently coming up with a salmon like some hairy crocodile. Those pools seemed to hold a lot of big dog salmon, which are two or three times as large as humpies. Therefore, with every catch she would have a twelve or fifteen pound fish to enjoy. She became very skilled at this and I always knew if I went down to the bay at high tide, I would find her there. The other bears congregated at the mouths of these small streams at low tide when it was easier to catch fish in the shallow water at the mouth of the streams.

These two stopped being a pair at some point that second summer, but I would still see them singly fishing the different tides. Both of them were fat and sassy at the end of that summer and had grown into that indeterminate age that marks mid-sized bears.

I still see them, or did as late as last summer. Blackie can still be identified by her scarred rump, and she still haunts the salt marshes at high tide. Blondie has grown into a magnificent male bear of perhaps eight and a half feet. He is much shyer than Blackie and I only occasionally see him late at night or very early in the morning. I suspect he has found superior daytime dining upstream somewhere, further from intrusive human observation. In a few years, he will be one of those great ten footers, but a particularly beautiful one with his bright yellow coat.

It has been fascinating to observe this pair over the years. I watched them grow from starving cubs that I doubted would survive their first summer, to the powerful animals they are today. I suspect Blackie will mate next summer or perhaps even show up with some cubs this coming summer, though I didn't see her with any suitors last year. She has reached the age of sexual maturity and I hope to see her with some cubs of her own in the next year or two. That will really complete the cycle for me.

The other bears in the area near my home seem to come and go. It is difficult to identify a particular bear because most of them are of the common color and indeterminate size. I rarely see any of the really big males near my home because these older monarchs are far too wary to feed near human habitations during daylight hours. Still, I occasionally see one of these monsters at long range. They are easy to pick out because their front legs tend to be bowed like a big boxer dog to carry their massive frame, while their heads look smaller in proportion to the big bodies. I am still awed when I see one of these giants even after all these years.

The years have passed and I still love this green island and its bears. I guess I enjoy their presence more now than I ever did. I still hunt, hike and fish throughout the year. I stalk bears with my camera. I still carry the physical scars and the physical limitations that go along with them. My left knee is weak and begins to shake after hiking or standing for a time. I have constant nagging pains that make a daily dose of

Motrin necessary. The oddest lingering manifestation is that many of the motor nerves in my upper face have never regenerated. When my mouth smiles, my eyes do not... People think I am unhappy or upset and they react differently to me than they did in the past. It took me a long time to figure out why and even knowing the reason, it still changes the social dynamic and as a result, my personality has changed. I am more withdrawn and introspective and more likely to avoid social contact. It is not because I do not like people, but simply because people are standoffish around me. I have adapted to that.

I have remarried since those days and my new wife is quiet and private like myself. We are loners together, sharing life with each other and a few close family and friends. My life has changed, yet I am comfortable and happy living that new life. I would rather be alone on a stream at dawn photographing bears than sitting in a coffee shop with a group of people talking about bears (or anything else). Maybe that was always true and that old sow just helped me find that out about myself?

I do not know the answers to such questions.

Perhaps that old sow is still out there, walking those hills to taste the sweet berries and dropping to the creeks to seek the rich flesh of salmon. It is February as I write this and if she is alive, she is deep in her winter sleep. I hope her dreams are pleasant and that in April she emerges with a new set of cubs.

Life is too short to hold grudges.

CPSIA information can be obtained at www.ICGtesting.com
Printed in the USA
LVOW05s1734031014

407168LV00028B/463/P